WORK DECISIONS IN THE 1980s

ELI GINZBERG
Columbia University

DANIEL QUINN MILLS
Harvard University

JOHN D. OWEN
Wayne State University

HAROLD L. SHEPPARD
Center on Work and Aging

MICHAEL L. WACHTER
University of Pennsylvania

 *Auburn House Publishing Company*
Boston, Massachusetts

Library of Congress Cataloging in Publication Data

Main entry under title:
Work decisions in the 1980s.

   Includes index.
   Contents: Introduction and summary / Nicholas S. Perna—Decisions
about employment in the 1980s / Daniel Quinn Mills—Demographic
changes and economic challenges / Michael L. Wachter—[etc.]
   1. Labor supply—United States—Addresses, essays,
lectures.   2. Labor and laboring classes—United States.—Addresses,
essays, lectures.   I. Ginzberg, Eli, 1911–
HD5724.W6415   331.12′042′0973   81-10860
ISBN 0-86569-094-4   AACR2

Printed and bound in Great Britain

PREFACE

Several years ago, the General Electric Foundation foresaw the growing importance of human resource and relations issues to both business and government in the coming decade. It therefore commissioned a series of studies linked together by a concern for how much time will be allocated to work during the course of a lifetime and the implications for both the workers themselves and society as a whole.

An analytic framework is provided for these studies by thinking of the U.S. labor market as a spectrum defined by the age of people who are employed or considering employment. The Foundation did not attempt to explore all aspects of this spectrum. For example, major studies of teenage employment and unemployment are already in progress. The transition from school to work is being urged upon educators as a major subject for their attention in coming years. Rather, the studies deal with the following questions: Should a person seek gainful employment or not? How much work is desirable? Should a person retire? At what age? For what purpose? Should a retired person seek a job?

Many factors affect the answers to these questions. Some involve the individual's own immediate circumstances: Financial status, family, and health. Others involve broader forces, particularly the large demographic shifts currently under way.

However, both the decisions and their consequences can be shaped by the policies that business, labor organizations, and governments adopt. Some corporate policies encourage early retirement, others discourage it. Some responses to changing hours of work can harm productivity while others will help it. Government programs and policies (for example, Social Security and tax burdens) also influence decisions about work.

In most cases, the chapters of this book are summaries of or excerpts from reports prepared by the authors for the Foundation.

v

As noted in the Introduction following, their purpose is not to present a single forecast of the work environment of the 1980s. Nor do they represent a "how to do it" manual for labor leaders, businessmen, or government policymakers. Rather, the chapters provide insights into the behavior of people during the past and direct attention to the challenges of the 1980s.

Certain areas have come into sharper focus since the research was completed for this book. The chapters point to the importance of productivity. Within the recent past, a strong national consensus on the need to raise U.S. productivity has evolved. In addition, the "supply-side" economists have significantly raised the level of concern over the extent to which high marginal tax rates discourage workers from providing additional labor. In one sense, the net outcome is not clear: Higher productivity would enable individuals to work shorter hours (or retire earlier), while lower tax rates could encourage them to work longer. In another sense, however, the results are unambiguous: Higher productivity means higher living standards.

Many people have spent much time on the project that produced this book. Special thanks go to Laura B. Salma for her editorial and research assistance.

D.Q.M.
N.S.P.

CONTENTS

CHAPTER 5
The Economic and Social Effects of Hours Reduction   107
by John D. Owen

INTRODUCTION

As the United States enters the 1980s, there is much uncertainty about what the future holds, but little doubt that it will differ significantly from the earlier decades of the post-war era. An optimist would probably describe this transition period as "dynamic"; a pessimist might call it "churning." In the following chapters we shall examine many dimensions of this impending change, in terms of both the overall work environment and individual workers.

The 1980s Environment

In the first chapter, D. Quinn Mills presents visions of the 1980s that might have seemed overly pessimistic a few years ago but may be more realistic today. For example, inflation is likely to be a problem for much of the decade. One of the most serious consequences of such inflation is that workers tend to heavily discount the value of private pensions at the same time that inflation escalates the costs to employers of providing them.

The nation's productivity slowdown is a complex long-term phenomenon. It worsened in the 1970s as U.S. firms utilized more labor than their European and Japanese counterparts in an attempt to minimize capital investment in an uncertain environment and to economize on soaring fuel and materials costs. Since U.S. factories are, by historic and international standards, "overstocked" with labor, it may be very difficult to reduce unemployment during the early 1980s. The United States has no choice, however, but to improve productivity performance if it wants to reduce inflation, reverse the slowdown in real wages, and regain a competitive edge in world markets.

Demographics and productivity, plus the added constraints posed by energy supplies and the battle against inflation, all add up to a slowly growing economy with very rapid structural changes. This creates all kinds of adjustment challenges and responses. Will workweeks decline substantially? Unions have increasingly opted for layoffs over work sharing in response to short-term slack, but they have favored spreading employment through fewer hours or days in response to longer term job scarcity. A number of scenarios are possible with respect to hours of work in the 1980s.

Despite an overall sluggish environment, the U.S. economy could experience labor shortages in the 1980s. Pervasive structural change means some bottlenecks are likely. During the 1970s, we were continually surprised with how fast the labor force grew. In the 1980s, we could easily be surprised in the opposite direction: Slow or negative growth in labor force participation could be piled on top of slower population gains. As the native-born U.S. population grows less and less rapidly, pressures for increased access by immigrants to U.S. labor markets will intensify. Moreover, industries that rely heavily on young employees will have to undergo a substantial adjustment process.

In looking ahead to a period of limited options, corporations and trade unions must endeavor to relax some of the constraints that would otherwise be binding and to simultaneously accommodate very diverse circumstances. For example, part-time work schedules may have to be considered much more seriously than they have been in the past. Part-time work can be used as a way of keeping capacity utilization up and as a means for accommodating the growing number of workers who are likely to continue to work beyond "normal" retirement age.

Implications of Demographic Change

In Chapter 2, Michael Wachter explains the "cohort overcrowding" theory of fluctuations in birth rates and labor force participation. When the Great Depression unexpectedly lowered living standards, young families adjusted by having fewer babies and more working wives. In the 1950s, however, living standards turned out unexpectedly *high* as the Depression cohort reached child-bearing age. There were relatively few of them and they were in short supply during the prosperous years following World War II. As a result, their incomes rose rapidly and they took some of the potential gains out in the form of larger families and slower growth of labor force participation. But this produced a baby boom that flooded labor markets a few years later. These new entrants adjusted to the surprisingly *low* living standards by a sharp reduction in family size and a big rise in participation of females. What will the new baby bust cohort do in the 1980s? The scarcity of young people will pull their income up relative to other groups (especially the maturing baby boom cohort) and relative to their expectations. This will lead to a turnaround in the birth rate (there were some signs in 1980 that this has already begun) and to a much slower growth of labor force participation (particularly among younger females) than was experienced in the 1960s and 1970s.

Less than a decade ago, government economic policies at the macro-economic level were perceived to be quite simple: There was a stable tradeoff, the so-called Phillips curve, between inflation and unemployment. Lower unemployment generally meant higher inflation. But something went awry in the 1970s: Unemployment and inflation both soared! The problem, as Michael Wachter explains, is that demographic and other changes (such as increases in the minimum wage and the availability of Food Stamps) pushed the "equilibrium" unemployment rate from 4 percent in the early 1960s to 5½–6½ percent by the late 1970s. Unemployment cannot be reduced below this level via general monetary and fiscal policies without triggering accelerating inflation. Any permanent reductions in the equilibrium unemployment rate can be accomplished only through "structural measures" such as training programs or by awaiting the reversal of some of the demographic shifts that are about to take place. Indeed, Wachter estimates that demographic factors alone will cause the equilibrium unemployment rate to decline by approximately one percentage point during the 1980s as the proportion of young people in the work force shrinks.

As for inflation, it is excessive monetary and fiscal policies that convert short-run shocks, such as large food and fuel price jumps, into long-run increases in the rate of inflation. Rising equilibrium rates of unemployment because of the demographic shifts gave the erroneous appearance to government policymakers of a lot more slack in the economy than was actually there. What was required was a period of relatively modest growth. What actually happened was a series of stop/go episodes. Excessive stimulation led first to accelerating inflation and then to recession, which reduced capital accumulation and, as a result, lowered the growth of the nation's capacity to produce.

At the same time, the massive demographic shifts brought about by the post-war baby boom dragged productivity down. In the cohort overcrowding view, this was not because the baby-boom youngsters were inherently less productive than their predecessors. Rather, the problem was that there were so many of them. However, while demographics explain most of the productivity slowdown of the late 1960s, they do not account for the further deterioration that began in the early 1970s.

What accounts for the slowdown of the 1970s? Other studies have emphasized insufficient capital formation and the explosion of energy prices. While Wachter agrees these are important, his analysis of the timing of the slowdown by means of specially constructed measures of *marginal* (rather than *average*) productivity suggest that the real worsening began in 1970 or 1971. This pattern would be consistent with an adverse effect on productivity arising from our first peacetime use of wage-price controls (mid-1971) and with the expansion of government regulations that began about that time.

What does this all mean for the 1980s? For the economy as a whole, labor force growth should slow, productivity pick up, and unemployment fall because of these "built-in" demographic forces. For the baby boom cohort, there are still some difficulties ahead in the form of relatively few promotion opportunities and lower-than-expected retirement incomes. But the next cohort, the baby bust generation, should find things much better. Its relative scarcity will translate into high relative wages. Smaller graduating classes should raise the return to investment in higher education, which has been on the decline.

Immigration—both legal and illegal—is one of the big swing factors in the long-term demographic outlook. Wachter attempts to shed some light on potential pressures and implications by comparing a forecast of labor *supply* (based primarily on growth of the native-born population and changes in participation rates) with the *demand* for workers by occupational category in the 1980s. The conclusion is that illegal aliens will be in even greater demand in the 1980s than in the past. A main reason for this is the demographic "twist" that is just now beginning to unfold. The replacement of the post-war baby boom with the baby bust cohort—coming on top of "normal" economic growth—creates sizable pressures for increased illegal immigration. As a result, the current U.S. system of quotas for legal immigration is likely to undergo dramatic change. One possibility is adoption of the European "guest worker" system whereby foreigners are granted work permits but not permanent permission to reside in the United States.

Early Retirement

The Social Security Act of 1935 seems to have "sanctified" or "institutionalized" 65 as the normal retirement age. However, present-day pressures are pulling in opposite directions. In Chapter 3 Eli Ginzberg focuses on early retirement, specifically the factors promoting retirement before age 65, as well as the experience of those who have retired early. As Table I-1 illustrates, there has been a sharp decline in the labor force participation rate of older males in the age categories on either side of age 65. (Female participation has been rising, but that's another story.)

Recent amendments to the Age Discrimination and Employment Act have raised the age at which mandatory retirement is legal for most employees from 65 to 70. Although this chapter examines the experiences of those who retired prior to age 65, both the findings and issues raised are useful in thinking about extending the normal retirement age.

A large number of the early retirees in the study remained in the labor force. Approximately 40 percent had done at least some post-retirement work and about 25 percent were working at the time of the survey. However, those who worked put in about half as much time as in their pre-retirement positions: 20 hours per week versus 40–45 prior to retirement.

Perhaps the most fascinating finding of all was that the vast majority reported that their post-retirement job was quite different from what they had done prior to retiring. The major complaint or disappointment: the impact of inflation on retirement income.

Table I-1 Labor Force Participation Rates*

	1947	1979
Males (16 and over)	86.8	78.4
55–64	89.6	73.0
65 and over	47.8	20.0
Females (16 and over)	31.8	51.1
55–64	24.3	41.9
65 and over	8.1	8.3

* Percentage of noninstitutional population in the labor force.

The prospect of continuing inflation requires novel approaches to maintaining retirement incomes. Cost-of-living adjustments are infeasible for all but a few holders of private pensions. Employees could increase their pension benefits through voluntary additional contributions during their working lives; companies might provide extra "retirement" income via part-time employment opportunities for older workers. Or we may even have to dramatically revise prevailing notions of pension adequacy and income replacement in light of the growth of multi-earner (and, therefore, multi-pension) families as well as increasing home ownership (and, therefore, increasing family wealth at retirement).

Employers may have to give serious consideration to offering part-time or flexible job opportunities to older members of their work force in order to accommodate both those who desire to retire early and those who wish to continue working past "normal" retirement age, to provide a source of income, and to alleviate potential human resource shortages as labor supply growth tapers off in the 1980s.

The present structure of Social Security benefits is biased toward early retirement. This public policy is costly in terms of both the benefits paid to early retirees and the decrease in national output due to their withdrawal from the labor force. The second of these costs—the lost national income—can be lowered by reducing or eliminating the decline in benefits that results from earned income.

A major challenge, then, of the 1980s is the utilization of the older members of the labor force who have both the desire and the skills to continue working.

Postponed Retirement

Although it also utilizes survey data, Chapter 4 by Harold Sheppard is very different from the study conducted by Ginzberg and his associates. Instead of asking *early* retirees about their recent experiences, Sheppard sorts through survey data for clues about the extent to which currently employed individuals could be persuaded to *postpone* their retirement.

Although Sheppard also examined other factors such as sociopsychological traits, the chapter in this book covers only the economic and demographic characteristics of the group of survey respondents who could be identified as likely candidates for postponement. What emerges is a large amount of variability across different types of workers, as well as some surprising insensitivity to factors such as pension benefits that are usually thought to be very important.

For example, workers in construction were least likely to postpone retirement, while those in the service industries were much more likely to do so. Differences by sex were particularly striking; for example, "candidacy rates" were much lower for females in manufacturing but higher for females in the finance, insurance, and real estate category. "Blue collar" workers were much less likely to postpone retirement than "white collar" employees; but in general the lower the current family income level, the higher the propensity to postpone retirement. The age of the worker seems to provide no explanation for differences in candidacy for postponed retirement. Perhaps most surprising of all was the finding that whether or not a male was covered by a private pension (over and above Social Security) made no difference at all in whether he would postpone retirement! However, women without pensions seemed more likely to postpone than women with such coverage.

Sheppard's findings strongly suggest that major future changes in private pensions or Social Security will significantly alter the composition as well as the size of the older work force in the 1980s. Whether these changes in supply (by occupation, industry, etc.) would be of the same direction and magnitude as future shifts in demand is a critical, but still open, question.

Length of Workweek

The final chapter by John Owen shifts attention from the length of working lives to the length of the workweek. As for the historical record, the "conventional wisdom" holds that the workweek has been declining rather steadily for many years. At the turn of the century, 60 hours was the norm. Just after World War II, 40 hours became the average, and by the late 1970s the workweek showed signs of approaching 35 hours.

While Owen's analysis confirms the big declines during much of the 19th and the early part of the 20th centuries, his data indicate that the workweek has really been quite stable in the post-war period. The "decline" in the reported average workweek for all employees over the past three decades is a statistical phenomenon.

It reflects the changing composition of the work force in the form of a large increase in part-time employment for women and students. For male non-students, the average workweek has been remarkably flat since the late 1940s. This is simply another manifestation of the demographic shifts analyzed by Wachter. The same compositional changes that have helped push the overall unemployment rate up have also pulled the overall workweek down.

Conventional economic theory is hard pressed to explain this phenomenon of decline followed by flattening. If workers typically choose to take some of the fruits of increased productivity home in the form of increased leisure rather than increased incomes, then why did they stop doing this in the post–World War II period? True, real income and productivity both slowed in the 1970s, but they grew quite rapidly in the 1950s and 1960s. While there are a number of useful explanations, the factor that Owen stresses the most is the interaction of the arrival of the post-war baby boom and rising educational levels. Since children and education both entail enormous costs over an extended period of time, any shortening of work hours and thus loss of earnings was not an attractive prospect.

What about the future course of work hours? Owen does not make a forecast; rather he presents several plausible scenarios that depend, among other things, on productivity prospects and demographic developments. For example, a continuation of slow productivity growth plus a rising birth rate (assuming the baby bust cohort does have more children than their parents) would prevent hours from declining. A sharp reduction in hours would require either very rapid growth of real incomes or a sustained period of very high unemployment, such as a replay of the 1930s Depression.

Owen also explores some of the possible consequences of reducing hours either through voluntary arrangements or by national legislation. A number of important effects—many of them negative—would emerge.

Fewer hours mean less output. There is little or no possibility that productivity would rebound as a result of lessened fatigue. While the fatigue factor may have been important when hours were being cut from 60 to 40 per week, it is hard to see how a further reduction to, say, 30 or 32 hours will yield significant increases in worker efficiency. There is every reason to believe that such a reduction would take the form of a movement to the four-day week, not a six-hour day, and there is no pervasive evidence that three-day weekends reduce fatigue. Indeed, Owen argues that decreased hours are likely to further reduce improvement in the U.S. rate of productivity for a variety of reasons.

Producing the same volume of output with a larger number of employees will tend to increase costs of recruiting and supervision. Fewer hours, that is, a shorter aggregate worklife, reduce the return to education. Since this lowers the incentives for employees and employers to "invest" in formal education as well as on-the-job training, it will lower the stock of "human capital" and thereby harm productivity. In addition, shorter workweeks would reduce physical investment in new plants and equipment by cutting cash flow and return on investment through lower capacity utilization rates.

It should be noted that shorter hours don't necessarily mean increased leisure. Suppose shorter hours are legislated in an attempt to "share the work." There's a good chance that many people would "moonlight" in other jobs. There's also the strong possibility that they would substitute "household production" (do-it-yourself home maintenance, car repair, etc.) for goods and services previously purchased from other sectors of the economy.

Paradoxically, shorter hours could produce a *decline* in recreational spending if real incomes declined as well. Studies indicate that this is because recreational spending is much more closely linked to the level of real income than to the amount of leisure time available. Even so, the manner in which hours are shortened is likely to affect the composition of recreational spending; for example, four-day weeks are much more conducive to travel than six-hour days.

Certain adjustments could reduce pressures for workweek reductions or offset some of the negative effects that would ensue if, in fact, hours were cut back. At the national level, maintaining full employment (through the appropriate monetary, fiscal, and other government policies) is a way of making demands for work sharing unnecessary. The experience from the Great Depression is that once such restrictions are adopted, they become permanent—even if full employment is restored once again. In addition, in the spirit of "supply-side economics," Owen points out that reduction of tax rates, as well as the adjustment of welfare-type programs, would improve incentives to work and thereby reduce the drive for shorter workweeks.

For private decisionmakers he stresses that work schedule reforms via "staggered hours," "flexitime," and increased options for part-time work could well be less costly responses to employee desires than are shorter workweeks and longer vacations. For example, they would enable workers to cut down on their commuting time (by traveling during off-peak hours, for example) and to more effectively combine work with family responsibilities without the adverse effects on real take-home pay, productivity, and output that would arise from shorter hours. In other words, *rearranging* hours may provide many of the benefits of *shortening* hours, but without generating many of the costs.

However, if hours are cut, then output will necessarily fall. But increased *shift work* could limit the adverse "second order" effects on capital formation and productivity due to decreased capacity utilization.

A Look at What's Ahead

The following chapters do not provide a "single scenario" of what the economy and the workplace will look like in the 1980s. Rather, they examine a large number of factors that will affect decisions about work in the coming decade. Whether inflation accelerates or abates, whether productivity climbs or collapses, will affect which issues assume the greatest relative importance. These features of the macroeconomic environment will also help determine the ability of labor, business, and government to respond to the challenges described in the remainder of this book. Given the high degree of uncertainty about the future course of the economy and the main economic variables, the key participants may have to spend more time than they care to sorting through responses and strategies that are "robust" enough to survive a variety of environments.

NICHOLAS S. PERNA
General Electric Company

Chapter 1

DECISIONS ABOUT EMPLOYMENT IN THE 1980s: OVERVIEW AND UNDERPINNING

by Daniel Quinn Mills

The United States has just had its first taste of the 1980s and now must ponder what lies ahead. What new problems will be encountered during the decade, and how will those problems already in existence be resolved? What new opportunities will be offered? How should business, the unions, and the government respond to these challenges?

Nowhere are the uncertainties and the likelihood of change more apparent than in the areas of human resources and the labor market. The American work force continues to change, both in its characteristics and in its attitudes, while the economic environment continues to evolve.

The late 1970s gave us a preview of the 1980s, and in some ways, the 1980s will simply be an extension of what we've already experienced. The decade has begun with a fairly typical business cycle: The recession of 1980 has given way to the recovery of 1981. What is not typical, however, is the enormous investment in energy facilities, in manufacturing plants, and in transportation systems that is likely to take place in the years ahead. The emphasis on consumption that has characterized the American economy in recent years seems to be giving way to a period of high investment, although some years will pass before high investment shows its payoff for the entire economy.

1

As a whole, then, the 1980s will tend to be characterized by slow economic growth, rapid inflation, and high unemployment. Economic circumstances such as these will cause problems as well as offer opportunities for managers and for the work force. Companies will face a challenging environment due to rapid economic changes, new technological developments, and new sources of competition.

By the late 1970s the share of total assets held by two hundred of the largest American corporations was steadily increasing. However, the degree of product market concentration—that is, the number of firms that account for most of the sales—was decreasing. These two developments seem paradoxical at first glance: Larger firms were controlling more of the economy, yet there was more competition. Apparently, the resolution of the paradox is that large firms are more diversified and confront each other in more and more product markets.

Large firms, operating in many different product markets and subject to a changing economic environment, are understandably interested in efficiency and flexibility in operations. At the same time, individual managers and workers, confronting growing performance demands from their superiors, are understandably concerned about their personal security. The confrontation of these two forces in the American labor market in the 1980s is a circumstance that will require careful analysis and response.

The Impact of Inflation on the Labor Force

Inflation is becoming an increasingly important feature of the American economy and is beginning to have a significant effect on people's decisions about work. The numbers are sobering. Consumer prices rose by about one quarter in the 1950s, by one third during the 1960s, and doubled over the course of the 1970s. In the 1980s, if current rates of inflation (13 percent in 1980) persist, consumer prices will triple (see Figure 1–1). While most observers do not expect current inflation rate increases to continue, it is becoming more and more likely that the 1980s will be a decade of double-digit inflation.

Such an economic environment is relatively new to the American population. One of the most devastating effects of double-digit inflation has been directed toward that segment of the population that relies on fixed-income pensions. Retirees are understandably con-

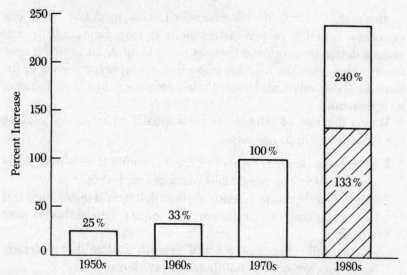

Figure 1-1 Cumulative Percentage Change in the Consumer Price Index. The shaded part represents the forecast; the full height represents the potential rise if recent experience continues.

cerned about their ability to survive. The indexing of Social Security payments to the rate of inflation has helped to lessen this concern but has not eliminated it. Persons approaching retirement, as well as those already retired, now seek indexation of private pensions. Others are deciding to postpone retirement because they believe they cannot afford to retire in such an uncertain economic environment.

Sheppard's survey in Chapter 4 of this volume shows that, on the average, people without private pensions were not more willing to postpone retirement. Conversely, we may expect that people with private pensions are no more likely to retire than those without private pensions. This finding is extraordinary and requires more investigation. It implies that with quickened inflation, employees now discount, and in fact disregard, private fixed-benefit pension plans when making retirement decisions. If this implication is correct (and it seems likely that it is) then the purpose of private pension plans is changing. Historically these plans have been supported because they provide a measure of security for employees in their retirement years. Employees are thereby encouraged to retire with some confidence that their needs will be met. Inflation is apparently undermining this important function of private pensions to the extent that their effectiveness is now in doubt. A second important function of private pensions is that they contribute to savings in the economy and thereby provide funds for capital investments. This function may be imperiled if employees cease to believe in their value and shift their preference to other forms of compensation.

Unless the rate of inflation is substantially reduced, we may be left with these three options:

1. A private pension system of fixed benefits that is essentially irrelevant to the needs and plans of employees.
2. An indexed private pension system that would imply high and uncertain costs for businesses and impair their ability to raise credit.
3. Virtual full reliance on a Social Security system that is already experiencing substantial financial problems.

The Productivity Problem in the United States

One of the most disturbing aspects of the U.S. economic performance in recent years has been the slowdown in labor productivity growth. Since 1960 the United States has had one of the lowest rates of labor productivity growth among the western industrialized nations (see Table 1-1). Slow growth in productivity has characterized both our economy as a whole and manufacturing in particular.

This does not mean that the United States does not still enjoy a relatively high level of real output per employee because it does. Table 1-2 indicates that in 1977 the level of U.S. labor productivity was still some 8 percent greater than in Canada and France, 15 percent greater than in Germany, and 31 percent greater than in Japan. However, as the table also indicates, the gap has narrowed since 1960 in each instance, and other data indicate that the margin continues to shrink.

Within the last thirty years, labor productivity growth has slowed dramatically from 4.2 percent during the 1947–1953 period to a mere 0.8 percent in the years 1973–1978 (see Figure 1–2). These statistics concern labor productivity only. Other measures of productivity, however, also show a slower rate of improvement in recent years.

Productivity is a complex concept, although it is defined by a

Table 1-1 Growth in Labor Productivity in the United States and Abroad

Country	Average Annual Percent Change	
	Manufacturing 1960–1978	All Industries 1960–1976
United States	2.8	1.7
United Kingdom	2.9	2.2
Canada	4.0	2.1
Germany	5.4	4.2
France	5.5	4.3
Italy	5.9	4.9
Belgium	6.9*	—
Netherlands	6.9*	—
Sweden	5.2	—
Japan	8.2	7.5

SOURCE: *Report on Productivity*, Council on Wage and Price Stability; Executive Office of the President, Washington: July 1979.

* 1960–1977.

simple arithmetic measure. Labor productivity is the level of real output divided by the amount of labor used to produce it within a given period of time. But virtually every aspect of our economy is interrelated and affects the levels of output and, therefore, the ratio of output to labor input. If sales decline, output falls off; then employees are laid off and productivity declines. If companies use more labor in order to reduce materials wastage, labor productivity

Table 1-2 Levels of Labor Productivity in the U.S. and Abroad, 1960 and 1977

Country	Real Gross Domestic Product per Employed Civilian	
	1960	1977
United States	100	100
Canada	87	92
France	61	92
Germany	56	85
Italy	40	63
Japan	27	69
United Kingdom	57	62

SOURCE: *Report on Productivity*, Council on Wage and Price Stability; Executive Office of the President, Washington: July 1979.

Index: U.S. = 100.

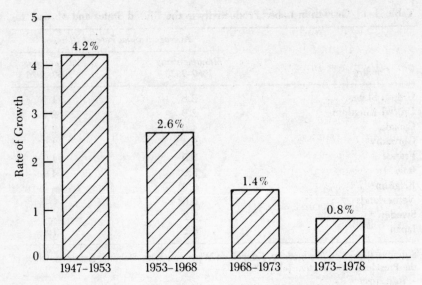

Figure 1-2   Real Gross National Product Per Hour

declines, although profits may rise—a phenomenon that may often encourage a company to reduce its average labor productivity. Finally, if employees work less diligently or are less skilled, labor productivity declines.

The productivity slide is a matter of great concern to Americans and has elicited many possible explanations. Two principal explanations focus on the role of employees and on the shift by American businesses away from capital investments toward increased use of labor. Because the slowdown is such a significant aspect of today's economy, we will examine these two theories and their implications for corporate and public policy.[1]

The Role of Employees

Explanations that stress the role of employees in the slowdown of productivity growth point to two different phenomena, one of which involves the supposed unwillingness of employees to work as hard today as they did in the past. Excessive absenteeism and "slacking off" on the job are among the problems that disrupt production processes and make them less efficient. The generally accepted belief is that today's labor force is less work oriented and more difficult to supervise. However, the degree to which these factors affect productivity growth is still in question.

The other explanation that stresses the employees' role in the slowdown of productivity growth involves the changing demographics of our labor force. Young persons and previously unemployed women now make up a larger proportion of the labor force than they did before. It is argued that these persons, on the average, are less productive than are older males. As a result, the economy is said to experience lower rates of productivity growth. Wachter, in particular, adheres to this explanation, concluding that for these reasons our economy has moved toward higher inflation and increased unemployment during the past two decades. He also holds out hope that in the 1980s the maturing of the post–World War II baby boom will result in improved productivity and lower unemployment.

Peter Clark tried in 1978 to estimate the impact the presence of more females and young people in the work force had on the declining rate of productivity growth. He argued that perhaps one quarter of the decline, from 2.75 percent in 1965 to 2 percent in 1973, was due to the changing composition of the labor force.[2]

Other economists, however, viewed this estimate as an upper limit. They pointed out that younger people are, for the most part, both better educated and healthier than their elders and are often preferred employees. They claim that hiring young people does not result in loss of productivity. They further argue that because women are traditionally placed in less skilled and less productive jobs, what appears to be the lesser ability of women workers is really a result of discrimination.

The Shift from Capital Investments to Increased Use of Labor

Clark traces none of the productivity decline to the changing nature of the economy. Again, other economists do not agree. For example, Lester C. Thurow, in a recent paper, attributes almost half of the decline in the growth rate of labor productivity to the shift from a goods-producing economy to a service- and government-oriented economy. Clark does, however, attribute much of the productivity decline to a lower level of investment by American firms.

In the 1950s and 1960s the growth of capital investment exceeded that of employment to such a degree that the ratio of capital to labor rose by 2 to 3 percent per year (see Figure 1–3). With a rising capital stock to work with, often embodying new technology, work-

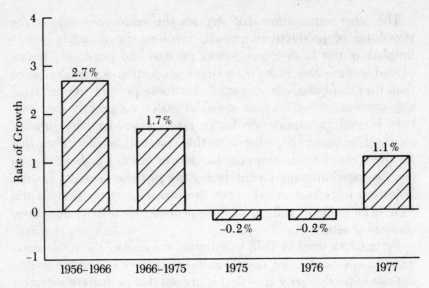

Figure 1-3   Growth and Decline in the Capital-to-Labor Ratio in the United
States

ers during this period were more productive. By the mid-1970s, the
growth of capital in the American economy had slowed markedly,
and in 1975, a year of deep recession, the capital-to-labor ratio
declined. By 1976 and 1977 it was growing again, but slowly.

In fact, in the mid-1970s American manufacturing firms were
cautious about capital investment, but relatively expansive about
employment. This attitude can be seen most clearly from the international comparative data in Table 1–3. In the most telling comparison, American manufacturers and manufacturers in France, Japan,
and Germany increased output between 1972 and 1978 by some-

**Table 1–3   Rates of Change in Manufacturing, by Country, 1972–1978 (in
Percent)**

Country	Output	Employment	Output/Hour
France	22.2	−2.2	33.4
Germany	12.5	−12.0	36.2
United States	18.6	6.5	11.7
United Kingdom	3.6	−1.1	5.8
Japan	21.6	−4.7	33.0

SOURCE: *Manufacturing Productivity Rates*, U.S. Bureau of Labor Statistics, Washington:
July 9, 1979.

what similar amounts. During the same period employment fell in France by 2.2 percent, in Japan by 4.7 percent, and in Germany by 12 percent; but in the United States, manufacturers *increased* employment by 6.5 percent. The result was a much lower rate of productivity increase (fully two thirds lower) in the United States than in France, Japan, or Germany.

Did American manufacturers increase labor, while Europeans and Japanese laid off employees? If so, this behavior was in great contrast to the behavior expected of them. For years, observers have spoken of labor as a fixed input in European and Japanese business and as a variable input in the United States. It is clear from the data in Table 1–3 that foreign manufacturers were treating labor as a variable, just as American firms were. However, American firms have been *increasing* their utilization of labor, thereby *decreasing* productivity, in contrast to what is occurring abroad.

Why have American firms used labor more intensively in recent years than have their counterparts in the industrialized West? There are probably two reasons. First, American firms have apparently minimized capital investment, preferring to add shifts and otherwise increase the labor force to give older plants and equipment more intensive use. European and Japanese firms have continued high rates of real investment.

The second reason is that Americans have apparently attempted to substitute labor for factors in production such as energy and materials, which have become relatively more expensive than labor. For example, in 1967 the costs of materials, energy, and transportation consumed 47 percent of the total value of shipments by American manufacturers; in 1976 this figure was 57.5 percent. In the same period, direct labor costs dropped from 14.6 percent of the total value of shipments to 11.6 percent.[3]

American managers have possibly found ways to increase labor and thereby economize on the costs of fuel and materials. Perhaps managers have neglected to minimize labor costs because their attention has recently been directed toward these other rising costs. Whatever the reason, the effect is the same: American managers have apparently maximized short-run profits and increased the return on invested capital by minimizing capital outlays in an uncertain environment and by utilizing more labor than they would have previously. A letter recently received from an American operations manager reads as follows:

I have been exposed to the addition of labor to maximize capacity and increase return on investment. Labor unit costs increase, but not to the extent of variable profit contribution from the sale of the additional capacity. Unit labor cost reductions are sacrificed for the larger incremental profits and avoidance of capital expenditure.

Why has this process not occurred to the same degree in Europe and Japan? It appears that capital investment has proceeded with a view toward longer-term profitability—a characteristic of European and Japanese managers in contrast to their American counterparts. This trend has often been cited in the literature on comparative international management.[4] Also, labor costs abroad have risen more rapidly than in the United States[5] and in some countries have outdistanced the costs of energy and material. As a result, labor has become a relatively expensive factor of production.

Future Implications

What are the implications for the future of these patterns of managerial behavior? By historical and international standards, American manufacturing is overstocked with employees. This situation has contributed to the comparatively low rate of unemployment in the United States. In Western Europe, American companies are now being cited as examples of social responsibility for increasing employment, while Europe suffers under a rising tide of joblessness.

Yet this halo of social responsibility hovers precariously over the United States. The low-investment economy of recent years now causes apprehension, and the government is being urged to encourage a wave of new capital expenditures. Also, slow productivity growth has itself become a target of concern, so that improvement in productivity may become an objective. If European and Japanese experience can be used as a guide, future increases in capital investment and productivity improvements will focus on balanced job reductions, not employment enhancement. In sum, the trade-off between improved productivity growth and employment looms to be both serious and substantial in the early 1980s.

Accepting low productivity growth in order to maintain employment levels is not a satisfactory short-run solution. More is to be gained, in fact, from the long-term benefits of improved productivity. Not only will improved productivity help to keep American companies competitive in the international market place, which now includes our own domestic economy, but it will also help to keep employment up in the United States. Improved productivity is a key element in bringing about an increase in the real growth of our economy. In addition, improved productivity helps to offset inflationary pressures both through increasing the supply of goods and by offsetting, to a degree, rises in production and distribution costs. Finally, productivity growth is the major source of real wage gains for all employees.

Thus the need to improve productivity performance in the American economy is all too evident. At the same time, however, we must discover ways to minimize any adverse effect in the short term on employment in the economy as a whole.

Adjusting to a More Sluggish Economy

Of particular significance to the rest of the 1980s is the view that a low-growth economy has begun to dominate U.S. economic policy. With inflation in the double-digit range, the policymakers appear to have chosen to sacrifice economic growth for price stability (if it can be obtained thereby). Thanks to a shifting mixture of relatively tight money and intermittent fiscal austerity, the U.S. economy hardly grew at all in 1979, declined during the recession of 1980, and—according to many observers—is likely to experience a recovery of rather modest proportions in 1981. We can look forward, it seems, to a period of slow economic growth and, as a necessary result, relatively high unemployment.

In Chapter 2 Michael Wachter has summarized the analytic model that serves to explain lesser growth and more unemployment as a response to inflation. He argues that changes in the composition of our labor force have caused the rate of unemployment at which prices begin to rise to go up. Wachter also says that the equilibrium, or nonaccelerating rate of unemployment, has increased dramatically over the last fifteen years.[6] In his view this increase is due to an influx of young and female workers into the labor market and to "a bottleneck of prime-age male workers."[7]

The potential growth rate of the American economy depends primarily on the growth of the labor force, additions to capital stock, and technological innovation. In the 1980s, a distinct possibility exists that growth will be sluggish in all three of these areas. During the 1970s, labor force growth was substantial, and it offset some of the slowdown emanating from the other two areas. This growth will be lower in the 1980s due to the aging of postwar babies. Capital investment and technological advances ended the 1970s at a relatively low rate by historical standards. If this decline continues into the 1980s, the potential growth of our economy in percentage terms will be no greater than that of the 1970s and substantially below that of previous decades.

We apparently look forward to an economy in the 1980s that will grow at less than 3 percent per year, on the average. It is likely to be an economy that experiences unemployment rates at roughly the same levels as the 1970s (see Figure 1–4). (The figure for the 1980s is a projection by the author of this chapter.) Smaller labor force increases and slow productivity gains will combine to offset some of the impact of declining real growth, so that unemployment should not rise appreciably above its average rate of the 1970s.

Structural Adaptations Made Necessary by Energy Shortages

Although the overall economy may perform sluggishly in the 1980s, there is almost certain to be a good deal of flux beneath the surface. Some industries will expand rapidly; others will contract. Not all

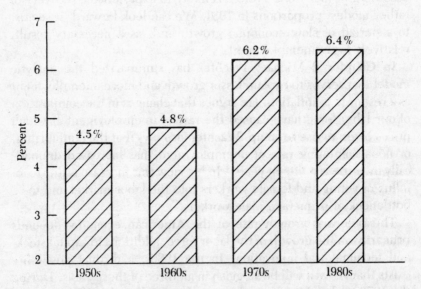

Figure 1-4 Unemployment Rate (Annual Average)

companies, employees, or localities will have similar fortunes, good or bad. The forces set in motion by demographic swings over the past quarter century and the shift to very expensive energy during the past half-dozen years will generate pervasive structural adaptations. While overall growth may turn out to be lower in the 1980s than in recent decades, the volume of change is likely to be even larger. No matter what the rate of total GNP growth, this pervasive change poses major challenges to—and requires significant adjustments of—the processes associated with employment decisions. Of course, the slower the overall growth rate, the more difficult it may be to deal with the resulting stresses.

James Schlesinger, former secretary of energy of the United States, in a speech in September 1979, described the economy of the 1980s as one in which a chronic energy shortage was relieved only by periodic recessions. We have a picture of a sluggish, though growing, economy. Furthermore, even if it should prove possible to secure enough energy to permit a more rapid economic expansion, and even if productivity advances more rapidly than is now anticipated, these gains might not translate into increases in real wages and real incomes. OPEC may, by increasing price levels for crude oil, continue to alter the terms of international trade substantially against the United States, which will prevent real income growth.

Work Sharing as a Possible Solution

In 1978 the Committee for Economic Development (CED) observed that the American labor force seemed to be splitting. A substantial number of persons had reasonably secure jobs; others were subject to repeated periods of unemployment and to jobs that were also in other ways, including pay levels and working conditions, inferior. Recently, Kim Clark and Lawrence Summers showed that about half of reported unemployment at any given time is accounted for by people who are chronically unemployed. Most unemployment, they conclude, "is characterized by relatively few persons who are out of work a large part of the time."[8]

The CED suggested that some form of work sharing should be used to try to alleviate this situation in order to avoid increasing social tensions. Several labor unions, foreseeing an economy with a prolonged shortage of jobs, have recommended a trend toward fewer hours of work as a device to share available work opportunity among the labor force.

Recent trends in the American economy have been ambiguous with respect to work sharing. Average hours worked per week, as reported to the Bureau of Labor Statistics, have declined from 40.0 hours in 1948 to 35.8 hours in 1978. But, as John Owen will show later in this volume, this reduction is primarily due to an increase in the volume of part-time work by women and students. For non-student males, weekly hours worked in the nonfarm economy have remained unchanged.

Part-time work is of growing importance in some industries and of decreasing significance in others. Durable goods manufacturing, mining, railways, and utilities make the least use of part-time workers. In May 1978 these industries had only 4 percent or less of total employment in part-time jobs. In the economy as a whole, in contrast, some 20 percent of all jobs were part-time (see Table 1–4).

Part-time employment in manufacturing has been relatively stable since the mid-1970s. For example, part-time employees rose from some 6 percent[9] of total manufacturing employment in 1975 to 6.9 percent by May 1978. In construction, however, the proportion of part-time employees rose from 9.8 percent to 12.6 percent over the same period.

Table 1–4 Part-Time Employment as a Percentage of All Employees, for Selected Industries, May 1978

Industry	Percentage of Private Wage and Salary Workers
All industries	20.0
Goods producing	8.0
Mining	3.5
Construction	12.6
Manufacturing	6.9
Durable	4.2
Nondurable	10.9
Other	
Railroads	1.4
Other transportation	16.5
Utilities	3.2
Wholesale trade	10.4
Retail trade	36.6
Finance, insurance and real estate	13.0
Hospitals	16.0
Education	27.7

SOURCE: Unpublished data from Monthly Survey of the Labor Force, Bureau of Labor Statistics.

As mentioned previously, some trade unionists have appeared to call for work sharing as a device to mitigate the impact of unemployment on workers. Some observers seem to accept this as the general trade union position; however, it is not. In the 1930s and 1940s many unions insisted on work sharing before layoffs could be made. By 1960 "the trend of union preference," wrote the authors of a major study of union policies, "is more and more toward the restriction of work sharing arrangements."[10]

In a recent article, James L. Medoff has shown that this trend has continued. Comparing the nature of hour-reduction provisions in major collective bargaining agreements, Medoff found a dramatic increase in clauses requiring an employer to initiate layoffs rather than rely on work sharing in response to a decline in business activity.[11]

Alternatives to Work Sharing

Will hours of work decline substantially in the years ahead? As usual, there are several crosscurrents. Slow productivity growth, combined with changing employee preferences, suggests that pressures for hours reductions will decline. Prior to 1920, increases in leisure for employees absorbed about one half of the increase in output per hour worked. By the 1960s, only about 8 percent of increased productivity was going into additional leisure.[12] Thus, the proportion of increased productivity in the economy going into increased leisure has declined greatly. Further, as we have seen by past patterns, productivity increases have dwindled to the point where the proportion available to additional leisure is negligible.

But will these patterns persist? Although unions have increasingly preferred layoffs to work sharing as a response to short-term downtime, they have also favored job creation when a long-term scarcity of jobs was feared. Thus, in the 1960s the so-called "automation" prompted the negotiation of severance pay provisions in many collective bargaining agreements. And in the 1970s prolonged employment stagnation in some durable goods manufacturing industries (especially autos and steel) prompted the negotiation of increased vacations, holidays, personal leave, and annual leave. These benefits require employers to maintain a larger work force than they otherwise would have needed to meet production goals. Where production has been maintained or has increased, employment has apparently been increased by these devices.

If we look ahead to a period of slow, total employment growth and outright declines in some sectors of the economy, several types of adjustments are possible. These options include an overall reduction in working hours, more part-time work, a reduction in the work year via increased holidays, vacations and leaves of absence, and increased work sharing. Each option has its advantages and disadvantages, but each is becoming more prevalent. For example, the state of California has recently provided legislation for an employer and a union to be certified by the state so that employees placed on a reduced workweek due to declining work opportunities can receive unemployment insurance benefits. Elsewhere, a worker must be "fully unemployed" to obtain benefits. This program may substantially increase the desirability of worksharing arrangements in economic downturns in California.

In Germany, some firms have been using an unusual alternative to layoffs during slack periods. Instead of laying off unneeded workers who may be difficult to replace when business picks up, the company in trouble lends its workers on a temporary basis to a neighboring firm in an industry where business is good. Firms in the American computer industry have sometimes lent employees to one another. And in preparation for negotiations with the basic steel industry in 1980, the United Steelworkers of America proposed preferential hiring rights for laid-off steelworkers at plants of other steel companies and portability of pensions between companies.

In Chapter 5 Owen points to possibly serious economic consequences of a shift to shorter workweeks if employers are thereby prevented from making optimum use of plant and equipment. Rather than leave equipment idle, Owen suggests reliance by employers and unions on multiple shifts and flexible workweeks, which permit plant and equipment to remain in operation.

Owen emphasizes that there are potentially lower cost alternatives to hours reductions. Probably he is correct. But a confusing factor has been introduced by Edward Kalachek, who notes that employers may offer a different hourly wage for workweeks of different length.[13] Kalacheck expects long workweeks to receive higher hourly pay, but he may be mistaken.

Owen identifies the following four scenarios for hours worked that might take place over the next several years:

1. Slow productivity growth and no significant change in average hours worked.

2. Rapid productivity growth and no significant change in average hours worked.
3. Rapid productivity growth and a sharp reduction in average hours worked.
4. Slow productivity growth and a sharp reduction in average hours worked.

Since the probable course of the American economy in the 1980s involves slow productivity growth, the second and third scenarios are unlikely. Furthermore, since inflation and slow productivity growth will squeeze the real income of workers, it is unlikely to demand greater leisure at the price of declining real incomes. For these reasons Owen's fourth scenario also seems improbable. Only scenario number 1 seems probable for the economy as a whole.

It is possible, however, that in some industries in which rapid technological advances occur, such as the introduction of robot machinery, substantial reductions in the workweek may result. These reductions, however, are not likely to be a pervasive or even widespread development in American industry.

Will There Be Labor Shortages in the 1980s?

Generalized labor shortages in the United States during the 1980s seem unlikely when we consider our expectations of a rather sluggish economy and the shift toward labor-saving capital investment. However, this is not to say that shortages in certain occupational categories, industries, and areas might not occur.

The Effect of Population on the Labor Force

The demographics suggest the proportion of the labor force made up of young workers will decline in the 1980s. In an interesting exercise, Wachter estimated the demographic composition of the labor force in 1985 if the demographic patterns in major occupational groups were to be the same as in 1970. Of course, by 1985 both the importance of various occupational groupings in the economy and the demographic composition of the labor force will have changed. According to Wachter, the result of these changes will be a shortage of managers, administrators, and craftspersons. These positions are traditionally held by males, and if they remain so, employers will have trouble filling them. Thus the shift of women into traditionally male-dominated occupations is seen to be, in part at least, a response to the emerging shortage of males in the labor force.[14]

The 1970s have seen very substantial growth in the American labor force (see Figure 1–5). (The figure for the 1980s is a projection by the author of this chapter.) Population trends in the United States suggest much slower growth in the 1980s—that is, about one half the rate of the 1970s. Yet population trends are not the only factor affecting labor force growth. In the 1970s the noninstitutional population 16 years of age and older grew some 19 percent, while the labor force expanded by 27 percent. "Participation" rose rapidly, as a larger and larger fraction of the population joined the work force. In the 1980s the working-age population will grow only about 10 percent. Participation rates could fall and cause the domestic labor force to grow even less rapidly than expected.

The Impact of Inflation on Real Family Income

Many observers have been pointing to the population's increasing disincentive to work created by the tax structure and rapid inflation. Periodic tax cuts have been able to offset only part of this disenchantment. Furthermore, the birth rate has begun to show signs of

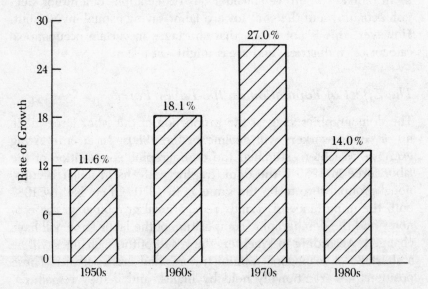

Figure 1-5   Civilian Labor Force Growth (Cumulative Increase)

increasing in the United States. Such a development would cause the participation of young women in the labor force to fall off.

There is an economic element to this situation as well. In the later 1970s, inflation caused real wages to decline slightly, on the average; but real family incomes did not decline. Rather, they continued to rise as more family members entered employment. An increasing labor force offset much of the impact of inflation on the family's income. In the 1980s, with slower labor force growth, the impact of inflation on earnings will be more deeply felt by American families.

How will families react to these harder times? Will more women seek work and the birth rate suddenly decline? Will belts be tightened and declining living standards accepted? For most people these decisions will probably not be made in the context of an individual but of a family unit. We know little about the factors that determine a family's decisions about employment by its members, but these decisions will be of substantial importance to the issue of labor force growth in the 1980s.

The Effect of Undocumented Workers on the Unskilled Occupations

Another possible area of shortages foreseen by Wachter is in the unskilled occupations. These jobs are held disproportionately, he argues, by young persons. The net decline in young workers expected in coming years will put special pressure on increasing the access of immigrants to these labor markets. The potential economic conflict between the low-skilled "native" poor and potential new immigrants is likely, in Wachter's view, to be one of the most sensitive political issues of the 1980s.

Proposals to deal with the undocumented worker have been made repeatedly in recent years. In essence, employers insist that any restrictions on the hiring or employment of undocumented aliens be accompanied by a reasonably effective system of establishing which potential employees are documented and which are not. For such a system to work, it would seem to require that American workers carry documents of some sort that would be reasonably secure from counterfeiting. So far, American political authorities have refused to take such a step, fearing its possible consequences on the civil liberties of American citizens.

Efforts to control illegal immigration at the borders are apparently having little effect on stemming the tide of illegal aliens. Consequently, illegal aliens are suspected to account for a significant part of the U.S. labor force, particularly in lower skill occupations. As the years pass, however, the skill level of undocumented workers can be expected to rise. Newspapers are already carrying accounts of small businesses and artisan activities being conducted by undocumented workers from families that are now in the second or third generation in this country.[15]

World population projections for the remainder of the century show substantial population growth in Latin America. By the year 2000, Mexico City is expected to be the largest city in the world, with a population of some 38 million people.[16] The expected inability of Mexican and other Latin American economies to generate jobs for their rapidly growing populations suggests that attempts by Latin American workers to enter the United States in search of job opportunities will increase in the coming decade.

In an environment characterized by sluggish economic growth and by pressure on job opportunities from undocumented workers, labor shortages will not likely appear in unskilled or semiskilled jobs on any but infrequent occasions and in any but isolated geographic areas. Nonetheless, many corporations will have to cope with imbalances in the supply and demand for employees that will be generated by demographic shifts. The imbalances are likely to be most significant as they affect employers of young people.

The Impact of Young People on the Labor Force

The youth labor market is a special one. Numerous jobs exist in our economy that seem designed specifically for young people. For instance, some companies hire school-age employees for part-time service jobs. Other firms have entry-level positions into which young labor force entrants are normally drawn. Some entry jobs involve formal training. There is, therefore, a readily identifiable demand (or employer) side of the young labor market.

Similarly, young people are an easily identifiable element in the labor force. They have their own behavior patterns[17] and labor force experience.[18] In the 1980s the number of young people will be declining as a proportion of the American labor force. Shortages may appear in jobs traditionally filled by young people. Michael Wachter suspects that, as a consequence, there will be pressures for the relative pay levels of young persons to rise.

The identification of labor markets that are specific to other demographic groups is not as straightforward, particularly as private and public efforts to lessen employment discrimination proceed. Yet the existence of a youth labor market, with the demographic twist that will be applied to it in the 1980s, is enough to imply a change in the overall structure of relative pay levels.

The Shortage of Technically Skilled Personnel

Shortages of technically skilled personnel for major projects in areas that are remote or that have not previously had work of the type in question are also likely. The manning of such jobs by national recruiting (now underway for the aerospace industry, for example) or by extensive training projects, which until recently accompanied the expansion of the nuclear power industry and now accompanies the advent of the synthetic fuels industry, is most likely.

The Relationship of Companies and Employees

As discussed in Chapter 3, 40 percent of the retirees responding to Eli Ginzberg's survey reported that they have worked for pay since they retired. While some retirees provided consulting services to the companies from which they retired, most entered new occupations, some of them quite interesting. The list included stockbroker, male nurse, economist, cabinetmaker, president of a real estate development firm, teacher, rancher, hotel manager, real estate agent, and priest-counselor. In many instances the retirees indicated they were much more pleased with their new jobs than they had been with their old ones. Many were now earning substantially more income than they had previously earned as middle-level managers.

The Mismatch Between Workers and Employers

The picture one takes away from these reports is one of a substantial mismatch between the aspirations and talents of many of these people and the job assignments from which they had retired. Large companies currently employ other people in positions very similar to the ones Ginzberg's respondents obtained after retirement. Why, one wonders, did the corporations and individuals involved fail to identify a possible complementarity between the individuals' changing ambitions and skills and the corporations' own needs? Instead, these persons apparently remained in jobs they no longer desired until they could take early retirement. Then they began the search for a new job.

The people in question did report themselves as satisfied, by and large, with the jobs they had held prior to retirement. This phenomenon is not, therefore, a matter of serious discontent but one of a lost opportunity for a better fit between corporate needs and individual ambitions. Described in economic terms, this phenomenon is a matter of lost productivity in the microeconomy. Only in the case of a few retirees does Ginzberg report real distrust for the company from which the individuals retired.

A second sobering finding about the relationship between employers and employees is reported by Sheppard in Chapter 4. Employees of many occupational levels were interviewed about postponing their retirement. Given incentives, largely financial, many would have done so. Only among blue-collar workers, both male and female, was there strong resistance to the suggestion. Put bluntly, those persons most directly involved in the production process in our society are also those most anxious to get out of it.

In recent years, considerable discussion has taken place concerning the role of producing and nonproducing groups in modern economies. Mr. Walter Eltis of Exeter College, Oxford, has argued that particularly in Britain, but also in Canada and the United States, economic growth and well-being are being smothered by the increasing number of nonproducing persons who must be supported by those who do produce.[19] His thesis reflects a concern shared by many thoughtful persons about the direction of our economy.

The Decline in Goods-Producing Employment

The shift of employment in the United States from goods producing to service and government sectors has been pronounced in recent years. In 1955, goods-producing industries (including manufacturing, construction, and mining) employed 40 percent of our labor force, as shown in Table 1–5. By 1975, the percentage was less than 30. By 1985, this author estimates goods-producing employment will be at 25 percent of the total.

The decline in goods-producing employment reflects a variety of significant factors, some of which include the increasing service

Table 1-5 Employment in Manufacturing and in All Goods-Producing Industries as Percentage of Total U.S. Nonagricultural Employment, by Year

	1955	1965	1975	Projected 1985
All goods-producing industries (manufacturing, construction, and mining)	40.4	36.0	29.3	25.0
Manufacturing only	33.0	29.0	24.0	21.0

SOURCE: *Economic Report of the President, 1979*, and author's estimates for 1985.

orientation of the economy, increased productivity in goods-producing industries, and competition from abroad in manufacturing. The decline has also been accompanied by much publicity about the alleged dissatisfaction of blue-collar workers with their jobs and the difficulty of hiring and motivating young people to do manufacturing work. Although often exaggerated, these problems do exist and will continue to exist. The Sheppard tabulations show that the desire of blue-collar workers to escape from their jobs by retirement continues, despite improvements in their earnings compared with white-collar workers over the past decade.

Corporate and Trade Union Policy

Many of the important decisions with respect to employment in the 1980s will be made by corporations and unions, acting separately or, on occasion, in concert. The policies they adopt help to determine the context in which individuals make choices. For example, the fact that most privately provided pension plans have fixed levels of benefits is a major consideration in employees' retirement decisions. Any change in the provisions of pension benefits might affect these retirement decisions.

Policy Choices and Trade-Offs

Many decisions by corporations and unions concerning pensions, layoffs, hours of work, and similar matters involve complex trade-offs. The advantages to employees of having pensions indexed to consumer prices are obvious; but the costs to employers are usually very substantial. Consequently, a choice must be made in balancing improved pensions against greater cost. The specific advantages to be gained and the costs to be incurred vary from company to company and situation to situation. Generalizing about such trade-offs is virtually impossible, other than to note their existence and importance. It is possible, however, to be less tentative about other matters.

Methods of Better Utilizing the Work Force

First, a substantial reduction in the average standard workweek in much of American industry in the 1980s would carry important disadvantages. If plants and equipment were increasingly underutilized, needed investment would be deferred because the return to capital would be lessened. However, there are certain methods of reducing work hours and simultaneously increasing employment that could avoid discouraging capital investment. Such methods obviously merit investigation.

Part-time work, for example, is now little utilized in most goods-producing and transportation industries. (The construction industry is the major exception.) Yet part-time work is the major device by which the average hours worked in the economy have been lowered since the 1940s and through which women and young persons have entered the work force in large numbers. Employers and unions in goods-producing industries and in transportation probably now need to reevaluate the role of part-time work in the 1980s. Such discussions have taken place in the automobile industry in connection with recent negotiations. Flexitime, staggered hours, and multiple shifts are other devices by which a work force can be efficiently utilized in a nontraditional manner. Until recently, the administrative costs of complex scheduling presented a major barrier, but the advent of the computer and subsequent cost reductions in computation have lessened this barrier substantially.

Second, the trend toward early retirement by employees in the United States is apparently lessening. Now that Congress has relaxed mandatory retirement ages, surveys show support for reduced work schedules for people over 65. Even by young people, there is strong support for moving the mandatory retirement age from 65 to 70. The Social Security Administration now reports that the number of persons age 62–64 receiving benefits declined in 1978 for the first time after a decade of rapid growth. The decision for business and labor is whether to encourage this development and, if so, how?

Provision of part-time work opportunities for older employees is a concept that deserves experimentation.

Finally, corporations and unions need to recognize different groups in the age cohorts approaching retirement. These groups are made up of the following types of people:

1. People in their current jobs with skills that the corporations can continue to utilize.
2. People with other capabilities that will show up later in other jobs or in voluntary activities after the individuals have retired from their current jobs.
3. People who are prepared to retire.

This third group further breaks down into (1) people who have adequate financial resources for retirement and those who do not; (2) people who have planned for retirement and those who have not; and (3) people who have special problems, such as deteriorating health, and those who do not.

Corporations and unions need to devise plans and programs to fit these differing groups of people. They also need to keep a better inventory of the talents and capabilities of their employees, so that as periods of technical and skill shortages approach, the existing resources can be identified and used.

Public Policy

In the same way that corporate and trade union policies create a context in which individuals make decisions, government policies create a context in which business, unions, and individuals each make their own choices. Michael Wachter argues in Chapter 2 that the government's economic policies for the past two decades have had a strong inflationary bias. Furthermore, government policies have failed to reflect the changing demography of the country. By underestimating the equilibrium level of unemployment, the government has overestimated potential real output.

The Effect of Government Policies on Inflation

The quantitative dimensions of the government's error are said to be substantial. For 1979 Wachter estimates equilibrium unemployment (the rate of unemployment at which inflation does not accelerate) at between 5.5 and 6.3 percent. Thus government's efforts to get unemployment in the 4 percent range seems clearly inflationary. Because the 5.5 to 6.3 percent range is an equilibrium rate, Wachter concludes that government cannot use the tactic of stimulation to lower the rate of unemployment below its equilibrium rate without inflationary pressures.

According to Wachter, the equilibrium unemployment rate has risen in recent years because of the influx of less productive workers into the economy. Also, the rigidity of wages against downward shifts prevents less productive workers from finding employment. At a measured unemployment rate of about 6 percent, today the economy is as tight in terms of real productive capacity as it was at a measured rate of unemployment of 4 percent in the mid-1950s.

In part, Wachter's analysis is important because it helps to preserve the fabric of traditional macroeconomic analysis. In the traditional analysis, slack labor markets contribute to a lessening of inflation. The roughly 8 to 6 percent unemployment rates of recent years indicate considerable economic slackness by post–World War II standards. Yet recent years have seen very rapid inflation. Wachter's response to this paradox is to try to show that labor markets are actually considerably tighter today than the measured rate of unemployment suggests.

This is an interesting argument and one that has contributed recently to the government's lowering both its estimates of potential GNP and its near-term objectives for the unemployment rate. But Wachter's analysis points primarily to what he calls the "intermediate" period in economic developments. This period is the time frame in which demographic changes are most important. In the short run, other factors are also significant in contributing to inflation.

In 1979, for example, rising interest rates, higher taxes, and rapidly rising gasoline and fuel oil costs contributed to much of the increase in the consumer price index. These price increases are not directly the result of an overheated economy. Wachter's analysis is not to be construed as a full explanation of inflation in our country, but rather as an identification of some contributing factors.

How Government Can Lessen Inflation

Wachter argues that government can lessen inflation by implementing the following kinds of policies:

1. Adopt tax measures that will encourage capital formation and thereby promote faster growth of potential output and productivity.
2. Reduce fiscal and monetary stimulus to levels that reflect a slower growth rate for potential output.
3. Accept a measured unemployment rate of 6 percent or so, while slowly constraining the money supply to reduce inflation.
4. Encourage productivity growth by minimizing the swings in GNP growth.

Certain policies will limit inflation due to domestic circumstances. These policies, however, say little about our response to inflation imported from the international economy. Further, such policies leave the economy with several million unemployed persons, along with the social difficulties that accompany unemployment, especially among minority groups and young people. The basic message of Wachter's work seems to be that there is no other choice in the near term.

But even as Wachter points out, the future is brighter than the past. Demographic changes in the 1980s will begin to reduce the size of the young work force. As a result, over the next decade the unemployment rate associated with reasonable price stability is expected to decline from the 6 percent range to the 5 percent range.

Other Public Policies Government Can Implement

While inflation is perhaps the most important public policy issue today, there are others of significance. First, the government should be careful not to force the reactions of business and labor into too rigid a format as a result of public policies. For example, mandating a reduction of hours in the standard workweek could possibly inhibit development of other work-scheduling arrangements that would be acceptable to employees but have fewer economic disadvantages. Reduction of hours in the standard workweek most likely implies a less efficient use of both capital equipment and of workers' skills and constitutes a wastage of existing resources. It threatens to further reduce the financial return to capital and to education at a time when increased real investment in equipment and education are both needed to offset America's declining productivity.

Second, government action, where it can add to the alternatives available to business and labor, may be justified on that basis alone. Thus, encouraging the establishment of part-time positions for the young, female, and elderly might help to increase job holding.

Finally, the question of the future of Social Security and its relationship to the overall system of pensions in the United States, complicated and controversial though it is, requires some resolution. Several years ago, Congress attempted to provide for the financing of the Social Security system for the remainder of the century. Yet on August 5, 1979, the Congressional Budget Office warned that Congress must again address Social Security benefits and funding as inflation and recession impacted the system.

In the 1980s, the growth of multicareer families will lead to multipension families. Increases in wealth are created by changes in government tax policy, such as in the forgiveness of capital gains taxes to elderly persons upon gains received from the sale of a residence. Increases in wealth generate more nonearning income. If, as seems likely, the current penalty in Social Security benefits for working wives is removed, earned incomes will also more fully supplement pensions.

These factors call for an evaluation of the distribution of benefits under the nation's patchwork pension system, and, in particular, under Social Security. The current system is becoming a serious liability because persons approaching retirement apparently discount fixed-benefit private pension funds; yet they are concerned that indexed Social Security benefits are also uncertain and are therefore also discounted. Consequently, the nation continues to accept high costs for a pension system that is substantially discounted by persons approaching retirement. Remove some element of stability in this situation and people will attempt to amass pension credits that are expensive in the present and heavily discounted for the future. For several years we have waited for a diminishing rate of inflation to resolve this problem for us. Now, possibly, the time has come to plan instead for continuing substantial rate of inflation and to adjust the pension system accordingly.

Summary and Conclusions

Decisions about employment in the 1980s will not be easy for the worker, the employer, or the government. The pressures from a changing economy and a changing labor force are apparent; the responses to these pressures are not. Here specifically are some of the key elements we can expect to see.

1. The 1980s will be a decade of sluggish overall economic growth, which will be accompanied by modest productivity gains and rapid inflation. Substantial variations will exist across industries and regions, with rapid growth in output, productivity, and jobs in some areas and outright declines in others.

2. Job opportunities in the goods-producing sectors will be stable or declining. The increased use of labor to avoid expensive energy and capital is helping to hold up employment levels in manufacturing in the United States, though not in Europe.

3. Manufacturing employment will decline as a percent of total employment, as will employment in all goods-producing industries. In 1978, the decline in manufacturing employment, which began in 1969, reversed itself briefly. The decline will probably resume in 1980. And in the mid-1980s, the decline will be reinforced by increased automation of many production processes.

4. The passage of time will give us a demographic twist in which the baby boom matures into a young adult boom. The proportion of the American population that is now of prime working age will grow. By 1985, far more people will be 20 to 29 years of age than 10 to 19. Thereafter, there will be many more people 30 to 39 years of age than 20 to 29.

5. Work attitudes in the labor force as a whole will strengthen. This change will be caused by several factors, some of which will include the increasing average age of the work force and the influx of documented and undocumented workers from abroad.

6. Inflation will continue to apply pressure to labor costs in goods-producing industries, but these costs will rise more slowly than the costs of other inputs (especially energy and materials) and the costs of other industrial nations. However, the increased competition from Third World countries will keep U.S. labor costs high, relative to competitors in many product lines. Diversification of large corporations, technological advances, and increased foreign manufacturing activity promise more competition in most product markets.

7. Inflation is having a significant impact on the decision of individual workers as to when to retire. With the exception of blue-collar workers, most occupation groups now show signs of ending

the lengthy trend toward early retirement. Surveys indicate that many managers who retire nevertheless remain in or return to employment status. Often managers work in technical or professional capacities that were largely underutilized, it appears, by the corporations for whom they previously worked. Retirement for many persons seems to be a way out of a mismatch of person and job. A clear opportunity exists for companies to make a more careful evaluation of employees' competence as they grow older and to draw on hitherto hidden talents for the benefit of both the company and the employees involved.

8. Adjustments to a high-inflation, low-productivity, low-growth economy have not been easy for either companies or employees. For the companies, increased competition and slow sales have caused pressure to streamline operations for greater cost efficiency. For employees, these efforts ordinarily have increased concern for job security. Where job security is enhanced by noneconomic practices, severe problems eventually result, both for corporations and for the employees and union involved.

9. The American economy has created a large number of jobs in recent years (9 million since 1975), but unemployment has only declined by some 1.8 million. This disparity between jobs available and the unemployment rate can be blamed on the increasing numbers of people who now seek jobs. For some age categories of the population, the number of jobs available are not relative to the need that exists. In 1979, for instance, the teenage unemployment rate was running some 17 percent (or 1.3 million persons). Estimates show, however, that if desirable job opportunities were available, a substantial number (some 2 million or so) of teenagers would accept jobs.

10. The American economy contains, and will continue to contain in the 1980s, a mixture of labor shortages in certain occupations, geographic areas, industries, and demographic categories. These shortages are in contrast to surpluses in other occupations, geographic areas, industries, and demographic categories. However, the 1980s will see shifts in the areas of shortages and surpluses. The most pronounced shift will be from a substantial surplus of young workers to a possible shortage of young workers. For those industries in which young persons now serve as largely unskilled help (including restaurants, farming, laundries, and other small service establishments), the labor market may become tight. In some

geographic areas this shortage may be offset by the immigration of undocumented workers.

No shortage of potential employees will occur for most manufacturing jobs. The age distribution of the population now is beginning to supply workers of an age that brings greater stability to job attendance and a greater reliance on income, as family responsibilities increase. For durable goods manufacturing, the potential work force is also larger, due to the inclusion of greater numbers of female and minority workers and the availability of large numbers of undocumented workers in certain geographic areas (particularly the West, Southwest and mid-Atlantic states).

Workers in certain skilled occupations may be in shortage, however. For instance, machinists, tool and die workers, and pipefitters are already hard to find. Persons in these occupations are working considerable overtime. Electronic engineers are also scarce. In some cities there are serious shortages of qualified secretaries. The weakness of training and educational programs for many skilled occupations will cause labor markets to be tight in some situations in the 1980s.

11. Recessions, layoffs, unemployment, sluggish overall employment growth, and competition from women, minorities, and undocumented workers combine to provide a very threatening environment in the 1980s for less skilled blue-collar workers. It is not surprising, therefore, that work sharing has again been raised as a policy objective by some trade unions and government officials. Work sharing could take many forms but has at its core the purpose of reducing the average hours worked by each employee, a reduction not seen in the United States since the 1940s. The decline in the Bureau of Labor Statistics series of average weekly hours worked by production workers from 40.3 hours in 1947 to 35.8 hours in 1978 is due entirely to an increase in part-time employment, primarily for young persons and females.

A substantial reduction in the average hours worked by the standard labor force could be very costly in the 1980s if this reduction took certain forms. In particular, a reduction in hours worked that caused substantial idleness for plant and equipment could add substantially to manufacturers' costs, while also reducing the incentive to make additional capital investment. Methods of reducing average time worked per employee that take the form of multiple shifts, flexible work schedules, increased holidays, or personal leave time, are, on balance, more favorable. These methods tend to be less costly, yet meet many of the same needs as reduced workweeks.

12. For the 1980s corporate personnel policies might seek to provide greater job security to employees and provide for more flexibility in job assignment and in career development (i.e., progress through different assignments). Corporations might also make better evaluation and use of the talents of older workers, seek greater selectivity in retirement practices, and provide more flexible work schedules as an alternative to fewer hours of work.

13. For the 1980s, government policy toward the employment relationship in private industry should support revisions in the Social Security system that strengthen its capacity to meet the needs of retirees at low-income levels, while minimizing costs through eligibility or tax policies with respect to higher income retirees (i.e., those retirees with a high after-retirement income). Government should also sponsor experimentation by industry and labor in methods of job assignments that involve part-time, personal scheduling, or other innovative devices that permit average hours of work to decline and yet preserve employment levels.

Endnotes

1. This matter is now being studied under another G.E. Foundation grant.
2. Peter K. Clark, "Capital Formation and the Recent Productivity Slowdown," *The Journal of Finance*, 33, no. 3 (June 1978), p. 974.
3. Data from U.S. Census of Manufacturers.
4. See, for example, Peter F. Drucker, *Management: Tasks, Responsibilities, Practices* (New York: Harper & Row, 1974), pp. 114–116.
5. Hourly compensation from 1972 to 1978 rose 70 percent in the United States; 87 percent in Germany; 136 percent in Japan; and 145 percent in France. (Source: U.S. Bureau of Labor Statistics, July 9, 1979.)
6. Michael L. Wachter and Susan M. Wachter, "The Fiscal Policy Dilemma," *The Economic Consequences of Slowing Population Growth* (New York: Academic Press, 1978), p. 72.
7. Ibid., p. 84.
8. Kim B. Clark and Lawrence H. Summers, "Labor Market Dynamics and Unemployment: A Reconsideration," *Brookings Papers in Economic Activity*, 1:1979, p. 14.
9. See Robert Clark, "Adjusting Hours to Increase Jobs," Special Report No. 15. (Washington, D.C.: National Commission for Manpower Policy, September 1977), p. 29.
10. Sumner H. Slichter, James J. Healy, and E. Robert Livernash, *The Impact of Collective Bargaining on Management* (Washington, D.C.: The Brookings Institution, 1960), p. 152.

11. James L. Medoff, "Layoffs and Alternatives under Trade Unions in U.S. Manufacturing," *American Economic Review*, 69, no. 3, pp. 388–389.

12. Juanita M. Kreps, "Some Time Dimensions of Manpower Policy," in Eli Ginzberg, ed., *Jobs for Americans* (Englewood Cliffs, N.J.: Prentice-Hall, 1976), p. 192.

13. Edward Kalachek, "Workers and the Hours Decision," *Work Time and Employment*, Special Report No. 28 (Washington, D.C.: National Commission for Manpower Policy, October 1978).

14. Michael L. Wachter, "The Labor Marker Mechanism and Immigration: The Outlook for the 1980s," *Industrial and Labor Relations Review*, 33, no. 3 (April 1980), pp. 342–354.

15. James Maker, "Ripped-Off by Aliens," *New York Times*, March 15, 1979.

16. "Facing the Future," Organization for Economic Cooperation and Development (Washington, D.C.: OECD, August 1979).

17. See, for example, Phyllis A. Wallace, *Pathways to Work* (Lexington, Mass.: D.C. Heath, 1974); and *Career Thresholds*, Vol. 6, R&D Monograph No. 16, U.S. Department of Labor, Employment and Training Administration, 1977.

18. See, for example, Kim Clark and Lawrence H. Summers, "The Dynamics of Youth Unemployment," in *Proceedings of the National Bureau of Economic Research Conference of Youth Unemployment* (Chicago: University of Chicago Press, 1980).

19. See Robert Bacon and Walter Eltis, *Britain's Economic Problem: Too Few Producers*, 2nd ed. (London: Macmillan, 1978).

Chapter 2

ECONOMIC CHALLENGES POSED BY DEMOGRAPHIC CHANGES

by Michael L. Wachter

This chapter focuses on the key problem of stagflation—that is, the high inflation, high unemployment, and low productivity growth of the 1970s and their implications for the 1980s. The first section presents the model of cohort overcrowding, which is used to analyze the changing demographic structure of the economy. Succeeding topics include stagflation, unemployment (in particular, changes in the "equilibrium" unemployment rate), the impact of demographic factors on the increase in the inflation rate, productivity slowdown, and the likely developments in the 1980s as a result of the ongoing changes in the demographic composition of the population. The final portion presents an analysis of the immigration issue, for immigration policy is likely to be of central public concern in the 1980s. It also gives an illustration of the general type of effects that can be anticipated in view of the changing demographic composition of the population.

Note: This chapter was drawn from earlier works including "Demographic Aspects of the Stagflation Problem," with coauthor Jeffrey M. Perloff, published in the Joint Economic Committee's Special Study on Economic Change, *Stagflation: The Causes, Effects, and Solutions,* vol. 4 (December 1980), pp. 168–192, and "The Labor Market Mechanism and Immigration: The Outlook for the 1980s," in the *Industrial and Labor Relations Review,* vol. 33, no. 3 (April 1980), pp. 342–354.

The Cohort Overcrowding Model

The cohort overcrowding model must be analyzed in the context of
the sharp swings in the fertility rate that have occurred over the past
several decades. Specifically, the current structure of the U.S.
population is a reflection of three dramatic shifts in the fertility rate.
The first shift occurred with the Great Depression in the 1930s. At
that time the total fertility rate declined, as did the total number of
births. The second major shift was the baby boom of the late 1940s
and early 1950s. At the peak of the baby boom in 1957, completed
family size had almost doubled from its depression lows of 2.1 children per family to a high of 3.8 children, with the total number of
births at over 4 million per year (compared to a depression low of
2.3 million per year). Birth rates remained high through 1962 and
then began a dramatic decline, which marked the beginning of the
third and most recent shift, the baby bust cycle. By 1976 the average fertility rate was approximately 1.8 children per family, and the
total number of births in the United States had declined to 3.1
million per year.

As a consequence of these three shifts, the age structure of the
U.S. population has become severely imbalanced. On one end is
the small group of under-16-year-olds in the "baby bust" cohort.
In the middle is the large number of 16- to 35-year-olds represent-
ing the "baby boom." Next is a small group of 40- and 50-year-olds
whose numbers were determined by the sharp drop in the birth
rate as well as the virtual cessation of immigration during the Depression. In the oldest age categories are the survivors of the cohort
resulting from the high birth rates and large influx of immigrants in
the first quarter of this century.

Neither a high nor a low fertility rate causes problems in itself,
since an extended period of either would eventually yield a stable
and uniform structure. It is, rather, the rapid swings in the fertility
rate and the resulting imbalances in the sizes of the different age
cohorts that cause major adjustment problems for the economy.

Components of the Model

The cohort overcrowding model has two essential components.
First, younger workers differ from older workers in their specific or
job-related training. In the short run, young, inexperienced workers cannot replace older workers who are better trained to perform

specific tasks. Thus, shifts in the relative supply of younger versus older workers in relation to the normal demand for the two types of workers will alter the wages, employment conditions, and upward mobility of the two groups. For example, when younger workers are in relatively short supply compared to older workers, their wages, employment conditions and upward mobility will be favorably affected. When, on the other hand, there is a surplus of younger workers (cohort overcrowding), their situation will be comparatively unfavorable: Unemployment rates will increase, relative wages will fall, and opportunities for advancement will decrease. Indeed, given the low "elasticities of substitution" between more and less skilled workers in the short run, the adverse adjustments can be quite large.

The second component of the model is that young adults develop aspiration levels based on the standards of living they experienced when growing up. Young adults not only expect to do as well as their parents, but also they anticipate some improvement due to the ongoing increase in real income in the United States.

The Great Depression Cohort

The interrelationship between the formation of aspiration levels and the inadequate substitution of younger for older workers in production can be explored by analyzing the sharp shifts in fertility rates that have occurred since the 1930s. During the Great Depression, the standard of living for young workers fell significantly. On the other hand, aspiration levels that had developed during the upbeat decade of the 1920s were relatively high. In order to maintain living standards as close to their aspiration levels as possible, young families had fewer children, and more wives entered the labor force. Since income was divided among fewer family members, income per person increased. In addition, since children are expensive commodities in terms of time as well as goods, lower birth rates meant more time available for family members to work in the labor force. The result was an upswing in labor force participation rates associated with the downswing in the fertility rate.

The Baby Boom Cohort

The end of the Great Depression and the beginning of World War II saw an entirely new situation. The new entrants into the labor market were the children who had grown up during the Depression. As a result of their parents' lowered standards of living during the depression, their aspirations were modest. Indeed, they expected to mature in a labor market with the threat of long-term stagnation and chronic high unemployment. Ironically, this cohort was very small, so that, while their expectations were low, the demand for this entering group of workers increased their wages dramatically.

In addition, the adoption of Keynesian economics after World War II meant that demand-related shifts, similar to those that occurred during the Depression, could be dampened by monetary and fiscal policies. Thus, the economy could escape from the threat of long-term stagnation.

The young adults of the 1940s and 1950s faced a favorable labor market. With living standards significantly above the aspiration levels that had developed during the depression, a sharp upswing in the fertility rate followed. In other words, families achieved their desired standard of living with one wage earner, so they could afford the time and expense of additional children. As the fertility rate increased, the rate of growth of female labor force participation slowed; women could now afford to stay home to raise the children of the baby boom.

The Baby Bust Cohort

The baby boom children grew up in an atmosphere of continuing increases in real wealth and per capita income. Their aspiration levels, therefore, were affected not only by the high standards of living enjoyed by their parents, but also by the idea that upward mobility was a feature of American life. As they entered the labor market, however, they found the conditions very different from those that they had expected.

Competing with a large group of entry-level workers, the baby boom generation found their relative wages down and their promotion possibilities reduced. As a result, newly formed families found they could not afford to have a full-time housewife raising 3.8 children. Either family size or aspiration levels would have to be modified. What followed was a sharp decrease in fertility rates and a sharp increase in labor force participation of younger women. Unfortunately, the induced change in participation rates served to aggravate the existing oversupply problem of young workers and further drove down relative wages. The net effect was the baby bust cycle, which began in the middle to late 1960s and has continued through the present day.

But what of the future? As the baby bust generation begins to enter the labor market, young workers will be in increasingly short supply. This will generate an improvement in their labor market position, and will result in wages well above those of the baby boom cohort. Given relatively low aspiration levels developed during the 1960s and 1970s, this cohort will find it much easier to earn high incomes and gain rapid promotions. The anticipated growth in relative well-being should encourage earlier marriage and childbearing.

During the next two decades, as the baby bust cohort moves into the labor market, the United States will revert to a condition of growing scarcity of young people. Although the financial aspects of this condition are likely to push the fertility rate up, the increased number of births cannot relieve labor market shortages much before the year 2000. In the meantime, the shortage of young workers, their resulting higher relative wages, and a reduced growth rate of the overall labor supply will have broad implications for the economy and will play a major role in defining the key economic policy issues of the 1980s.

An Overview of the Stagflation Problem

In public debate, accelerating inflation, rising unemployment, and declining real growth rates are frequently viewed as manifestations of the same problem. The interrelationships among these variables, however, are highly complex. During short-run business cycle swings, stimulative monetary and fiscal policies increase the rate of inflation. According to Okun's law, there is a short-run relationship between real growth and unemployment; and a short-run trade-off has been posted between lower unemployment rates and higher inflation—the so-called Phillips curve.

Paradoxes Between Short- and Long-Run Interrelationships

The stagflation discussion, however, rejects these short-run relationships and concentrates on a longer-run perspective. The data indicate that between 1969 and 1979 the performance of the economy, as measured by any of these three variables—accelerating inflation, rising unemployment, and declining real growth rates—worsened. Slower real growth and higher unemployment have been accompanied by a threefold increase in the rate of inflation. Moreover, the supposedly stable "Okun's law" coefficient that links output and unemployment has been rising—a symptom of decreasing productivity growth. Lower productivity growth means that more employees or manhours are needed to produce any given level of output. It also means that a given change in real output is now associated with a larger swing in unemployment than previously.

The widely accepted negative short-run relationship between unemployment and inflation needs to be reconciled with the long-run stagflation picture in which unemployment and inflation have increased together. In addition, the relationship, if any, between the adverse unemployment and inflation developments and the declining productivity growth rate should be explored.

It would seem as if the paradoxes between the short- and long-run interrelationships involving real economic growth (or productivity), unemployment, and inflation are due in part to a failure to recognize the influence of intermediate-run swings in the economy. Whereas the short-run fluctuations are geared to the traditional business cycle, the intermediate-run fluctuations are related mainly to the impact of the demographic changes that involve the baby boom cohort.

In the context of these intermediate demographic swings, the stagflation problem is best divided into three component parts: real economic growth (or productivity), inflation, and unemployment. Although these three variables stem from similar causes that will respond to a unified set of policies, they also have distinctive characteristics that require separate treatment. The central element behind many of the developments in the changing relationship among growth, inflation, and unemployment is demographic change in the labor force and population. Hence, the focus of this chapter is on the importance of the intermediate-run factors and their impact on the stagflation question. Since my earlier papers have dealt with unemployment and inflation problems, this chapter devotes more attention to the *interrelationships* among these three variables, especially the productivity component.

The Problem of Secularly Rising Inflation Rates

One implication of the cohort overcrowding model is that the secular increase in the unemployment rate over the past two decades has been only indirectly related to the slowdown in productivity. As a consequence of cohort overcrowding, the current high levels of unemployment are largely due to the change in the sustainable (or equilibrium) rates and not to inadequate demand. Policies to lower this type of unemployment, such as job training and employment tax credits, need not have any effect on the rate of real growth of the economy or on the rate of inflation.

The problem of secularly rising inflation rates has been due largely to the failure of government policy. Of particular concern has been the tendency of policymakers to systematically underestimate the sustainable unemployment rate and overestimate the potential output of the economy. The target of 4 percent aggregate unemployment was maintained through the mid-1970s. A target unemployment rate of approximately 5 percent was finally accepted by policymakers only after the empirical evidence suggested that the sustainable rate was actually closer to 6 percent.

In other words, since the sustainable rate was being driven upward largely by demographic forces, the secular increase in unemployment would have occurred regardless of the government's aggregate demand policies. The linkage between rising inflation and unemployment rates has thus been political and not economic— that is, government has failed to recognize the limitations of monetary and fiscal policies in dealing with the intermediate-run trends in the unemployment rate.

Linkages between high inflation rates and slow productivity growth are also likely to be indirect and based on institutional rigidities. For example, higher inflation rates have created distortions in the tax structure that have, on balance, decreased the rate of return on business-fixed investment and hence slowed productivity growth. High growth and high inflation rates need not be mutually exclusive, as shown by numerous countries that combine high real growth and high inflation rates and others that combine *high* real growth and *low* inflation rates.

The Issue of Slow Real Growth

An additional theme of this chapter is to make clear that the productivity decline did not begin until the 1970s, although economists usually identify 1965 as the initial year of the decline. The appearance of a slowdown in the aggregate productivity rate between 1965 and 1973 is due largely to the impact of the baby boom cohort entering the labor market and the sharp increase in the female labor force participation rate. Adjusting for the age and sex characteristics of the labor force bears this theory out and makes the decline in productivity during the 1970s even more dramatic than the published numbers indicate.

The issue of slow real growth is a major concern and is the core of the stagflation problem. As discussed later, the exact underlying causes of the productivity slowdown are difficult to identify, but any general policy approach to increasing growth should be based on increasing the incentives to invest in physical and human capital.

In the short run, aggregate demand policies have allowed policymakers to expand the economy, reduce unemployment, and increase real GNP growth. The only costs have been higher rates of inflation. The problem is that in the long run the economy is left with the legacy of higher and higher inflation. Keynesian policies can neither permanently lower unemployment below its equilibrium rate nor permanently increase the real rate of economic growth.

The Rise in Unemployment

The high level of unemployment that existed in the 1970s was due largely to changes in the equilibrium level of unemployment and not to the lack of aggregate demand. Estimates of the equilibrium level of unemployment suggest that the U.S. economy fully recovered from the 1974–1975 recession by late 1978 and began experiencing excess demand conditions during 1979, at a time when the unemployment rate hovered around 6 percent. The short 1980 recession pushed unemployment above 7.5 percent that year.

Equilibrium unemployment rate, as used in this paper, is defined as that rate of unemployment that cannot be reduced by general monetary and fiscal policies without further accelerating inflation. Structural measures, however, such as job training and employment tax credits, in combination with the demographic outlook in the 1980s, may be successful in reducing the equilibrium unemployment rate.

This chapter uses two alternative approaches for estimating the equilibrium unemployment rate (denoted by U^*) The first approach, U^*_1, is based on adjustments both for changes in the demographic composition of the labor force and for government transfer programs. The second approach, U^*_2, is derived by inverting a wage or price equation for that level of the unemployment rate compatible with nonaccelerating inflation.

Estimating U^* by Adjusting for Demographic and Institutional Changes

Adjusting the equilibrium, or full-employment/unemployment rate for changes in the demographic composition of the labor force is now a widely accepted procedure. The aggregate rate of unemployment can be viewed as a weighted average of two component rates—a low rate for prime-age workers and a high rate for younger workers—where the relative weights are based on the proportion that the two groups represent in the work force. The high rate of unemployment for younger workers reflects their inexperience in the labor market, their job-seeking activity, and the tentativeness of their job commitments. Without any change in the unemployment rate for either group, a rise in the proportion of youths in the labor force will raise the overall unemployment rate.

If the equilibrium unemployment rate were 4 percent in 1955, then, as a result of these changing relative weights alone, the rate would be approximately 5.1 percent today. If the equilibrium unemployment rates for each age-sex group were the same in both 1955 and 1979, the nationwide equilibrium unemployment rate would be 1.1 percent higher by 1979. This increase would be due solely to the relative increase in the number of younger workers, a group that has a high incidence of unemployment. The data suggest, however, that the increase in U^* over the past twenty-five years has been greater than 1.1 percent. The reason is that the equilibrium unemployment rates for the younger group have increased over time.

Demographic Changes. Due to wage rigidities and the fact that young and old workers are imperfect substitutes for each other, an influx of younger workers creates overcrowding in the jobs typically held by them. One effect of the demographic overcrowding is a dramatic fall in relative wages for younger workers, as indicated in Tables 2–1 and 2–2. These tables show the income of workers in each of the age-sex groups relative to the income of prime-age males, 45 to 54 years old. For example, while males 20 to 24 years old earned $73 for every $100 earned by prime-age males in 1955, they earned only $58 for every $100 in 1977.

Table 2–1   Relative Wages for Males 1955–1977

	Cohort Age Groups						
Year	14–19	20–24	25–34	35–44	45–54	55–64	65+
1955	.4084	.7331	.9593	1.0049	1.0	.8816	.6698
1956	.4159	.7465	.9664	1.0473	1.0	.8878	.7397
1957	.3274	.7078	.9583	1.0205	1.0	.8641	.6808
1958	.3541	.6687	.9747	1.0400	1.0	.9119	.6879
1959	.3222	.6889	.9850	1.0626	1.0	.9304	.7363
1960	.3477	.6897	.9598	1.0403	1.0	.8945	.7247
1961	.3293	.6871	.9606	1.0515	1.0	.9908	.6830
1962	.3500	.6793	.9416	1.0533	1.0	.9052	.7255
1963	.3537	.6735	.9680	1.0677	1.0	.9309	.7423
1964	.3592	.6592	.9540	1.0588	1.0	.9157	.6987
1965	.4495	.6882	.9557	1.0524	1.0	.9196	.7458
1966	.3271	.6813	.9369	1.0495	1.0	.9028	.7274
1967	.3459	.6766	.9266	1.0289	1.0	.8947	.6990
1968	.3236	.6776	.9389	1.0479	1.0	.9134	.7148
1969	.3385	.6628	.9324	1.0342	1.0	.9024	.7071
1970	.3977	.6701	.9189	1.0329	1.0	.9134	.6801
1971	.3433	.6244	.8874	1.0287	1.0	.9013	.6772
1972	.3568	.5928	.8724	1.0123	1.0	.9090	.6552
1973	.3752	.5858	.8878	1.0120	1.0	.9194	.6995
1974	.3805	.5865	.8672	1.0056	1.0	.9039	.7066
1975	.3820	.5754	.8628	.9947	1.0	.9126	.7782
1976	.3535	.5632	.8333	.9877	1.0	.9263	.7381
1977	.3548	.5755	.8297	.9903	1.0	.9201	.8121

SOURCE: *Money Income of Families and Persons in the United States,* Current Population Reports, U.S. Department of Commerce, Bureau of the Census, Series P–60, various issues.

Note: Normalized on the male 45–54 group-based income data of full-time, year-round workers.

Institutional Changes.   In a perfectly competitive labor market, cohort overcrowding need not cause relative unemployment rates to change. Rather, relative wages would decline for groups in excess supply, and firms would be encouraged to substitute cheaper inputs for the more expensive inputs. In addition, products that use more of the cheaper inputs would decline in relative price, and consumers would be encouraged to use relatively more of those goods and services. Indeed, relative wages in the perfectly competitive markets would continue to drop until the victims of cohort overcrowding were absorbed into new jobs.

But there have been several institutional and policy developments that have occurred during the 1960s and 1970s which inter-

Table 2–2   Relative Wages for Females, 1955–1977

Year	Cohort Age Groups						
	14–19	20–24	25–34	35–44	45–54	55–64	65+
1955	.5093	.6151	.6342	.6351	.6220	.5687	.4004
1956	.4742	.5728	.6596	.6173	.6173	.5845	.4044
1957	.4599	.5755	.6375	.6021	.6097	.5824	.3995
1958	.4555	.5636	.6110	.6291	.6139	.5996	.4425
1959	.4351	.5693	.6288	.6034	.6088	.5880	.4196
1960	.4315	.5557	.6250	.5995	.5805	.5768	.4998
1961	.3895	.5339	.6112	.6040	.5634	.5645	.3960
1962	.4458	.5188	.5901	.5727	.5900	.5754	.4268
1963	.4671	.5260	.5956	.5899	.5907	.5805	.3953
1964	.4300	.5407	.5915	.5843	.5735	.5558	.4495
1965	.4108	.5430	.5936	.5956	.5775	.5736	.4525
1966	.3821	.5136	.5612	.5599	.5664	.5497	.4567
1967	.3728	.5057	.5720	.5571	.5662	.5429	.4383
1968	.3691	.5046	.5909	.5579	.5579	.5586	.4486
1969	.3659	.4994	.5751	.5626	.5697	.5536	.5055
1970	.3809	.4962	.5964	.5569	.5627	.5507	.4918
1971	.3272	.4846	.5777	.5399	.5417	.5455	.4671
1972	.3163	.4528	.5664	.5292	.5231	.5135	.4840
1973	.3042	.4335	.5555	.5317	.5231	.5164	.4359
1974	.3299	.4456	.5619	.5481	.5401	.5352	.5131
1975	.3085	.4456	.5673	.5459	.5389	.5257	.4881
1976	.3276	.4384	.5626	.5497	.5379	.5319	.5414
1977	.3307	.4402	.5604	.5451	.5368	.5195	.4654

SOURCE: *Money Income of Families and Persons in the United States*, Current Population Reports, U.S. Department of Commerce, Bureau of the Census, Series P-60, various issues.

Note: Normalized on the female 45–54 group-based income data of full-time, year-round workers.

fere with the competitive market mechanisms. Perhaps most important is the increase in alternative sources of income for nonworkers. Since family income has increased overall, less pressure has been exerted on younger workers to take low-wage jobs. Instead, young people have devoted additional time to schooling, job search, or leisure. The increase in the "reservation wage," the wage at which work becomes worthwhile relative to other activities, places a floor on the market wage. More jobs would be created for younger workers if the wage declined below the reservation wage, but these jobs would go unfilled. Obviously, the younger people from wealthier families would be most affected by this development.

For poorer individuals and families, the liberalization of transfer payment programs has had a similar effect in that they contribute to an increase in overall family income. Essentially, the expansion of the AFDC program, food stamps, and unemployment compensation have all served to decrease the "cost" of being unemployed.

Changes in government programs have affected younger workers in several ways. For example, younger workers living at home may jeopardize the ability of their families to receive certain welfare benefits if they work. In the case of younger workers establishing their own families, the more they consider benefits "liberal" relative to the market wage, the less they are likely to work. In addition, the increase in work registration rules for transfer eligibility increases the likelihood that workers will report themselves as being unemployed rather than as being out of the labor force, so they can still collect their benefits. Hence demographic overcrowding, by reducing the market wage for younger workers relative to the implicit welfare wage rate for unemployed workers, has resulted in increases in the unemployment rate.

While the increase in the reservation wage or the decrease in the cost of being unemployed may have reduced the number of younger workers willing to work at low wages, changes in the minimum wage law may have reduced the demand for low-wage workers. Of particular importance were the extension of coverage granted to the retail-wholesale and service sectors in 1967 and the gradual reduction in the number of special exemptions for low-wage industries over this same period. Although the level of the minimum wage itself has remained a nearly constant percentage of the economy-wide market wage, it has become increasingly relevant for younger workers. Due to the effects of demographic overcrowding, the wage of younger workers has declined relative to the overall market wage and, hence, relative to the minimum wage.

By increasing the equilibrium unemployment rates for the younger age-sex groups, these institutional factors—alternate sources of income, liberalization of transfer payments, and changes in the minimum wage law—have raised the equilibrium unemployment rate above the 5.1 percent level. One method of estimating the magnitude of this increase is to assume that the equilibrium rate for prime-age workers has remained unchanged and to view the changes in the relative unemployment rates that coincide with the rise in the proportion of younger workers as a measure of the increase in the equilibrium unemployment rate for the younger groups. This methodology yields an aggregate U^*_1 of 5.5 percent in

1979. The changes in $U*_1$ between 1955 and 1978 are shown in Table 2–3. The changes in $U*_1$ for the respective age-sex groups between 1955 and 1978 are presented in Table 2–4.

Recent observations however, suggest that 5.5 percent may be an *underestimate* of the equilibrium unemployment rate because as calculated above it is adjusted solely for demographic shifts. In addition to changing labor market factors, numerous other variables, including such diverse elements as the slowdown in the trend rate of productivity growth and changes in the terms of trade, also may effect the equilibrium unemployment rate.

One indication that $U*$ may be above 5.5 percent is the shifting relationship that exists between capacity utilization and the unemployment rate. For any given unemployment rate today, capacity utilization is apparently much higher than it was in the 1960s. The availability of labor was the constraining factor in the 1960s; now the availability of capital is the constraining factor. For example, inflation in the Wharton model tends to accelerate when capacity utilization is around 93 percent. Capacity utilization in 1979, however, was 93 percent, and unemployment was 5.8 percent—that is, the accelerating inflation point on the capacity utilization rate will be reached when the unemployment rate is still 5.8 percent. That is not to say that 5.8 percent is the equilibrium rate of unemployment.

Table 2–3 Equilibrium Unemployment Rate, $U*_1$ (in Percent)

Year	$U*_1$	Year	$U*_1$
1955	3.96	1967	4.77
1956	3.99	1968	4.81
1957	4.01	1969	4.91
1958	4.03	1970	5.03
1959	4.10	1971	5.16
1960	4.18	1972	5.29
1961	4.22	1973	5.39
1962	4.23	1974	5.42
1963	4.34	1975	5.44
1964	4.46	1976	5.47
1965	4.60	1977	5.48
1966	4.72	1978	5.48

SOURCE: Michael L. Wachter, "The Changing Cyclical Responsiveness of Wage Inflation over the Postwar Period," *Brookings Paper on Economic Activity* (1:1976), pp. 115–159.
Note: The equilibrium unemployment rates have been updated to reflect the latest available data.

Table 2–4   Equilibrium Unemployment Rate by Age and Sex, $U*_1$ (in Percent)

Age-Sex	1955	1965	1975	1978
Male				
16–17	11.14	15.15	17.92	17.68
18–19	10.34	12.03	13.07	12.99
20–24	6.35	7.34	7.94	7.89
25–34	3.03	3.37	3.56	3.55
35–44	2.71	2.57	2.49	2.50
45–54	3.06	2.66	2.46	2.48
55–64	3.70	3.08	2.79	2.81
65+	3.55	3.56	3.57	3.57
Female				
16–17	11.78	15.76	18.48	18.25
18–19	8.53	12.51	15.41	15.16
20–24	5.57	7.59	8.98	8.86
25–34	4.71	5.65	6.25	6.20
35–44	3.78	4.32	4.65	4.62
45–54	3.29	3.53	3.67	3.66
55–64	3.26	3.16	3.10	3.11
65+	2.39	3.06	3.50	3.47

SOURCE: Michael L. Wachter, "The Demographic Impact on Unemployment: Past Experience and the Outlook for the Future," *Demographic Trends and Full Employment*, National Commission for Manpower Policy, Special Report No, 12, December 1976, pp. 27–99.

But the capacity numbers do suggest that the demographic adjustment may be too optimistic.

Estimating *U** by a Wage or Price Equation

The second approach to estimating $U*$ is to estimate a wage or price equation and then solve it for the unemployment rate that is compatible with stability in the inflation rate. The resulting series $U*_2$ shown in Figure 2–1, is always higher than $U*_1$. Numerous alternative $U*$-type series can be estimated by altering the specification of the wage or price equation. The series depicted in Figure 2–1 is at a low end of the various estimates we obtained.

Much of the difference between $U*_1$ and $U*_2$ results from the more rapid growth of the latter during the 1960s. Since that decade reflects the strongest demographic impact of the baby boom, the possibility exists that $U*_1$ understates the impact of this factor. In

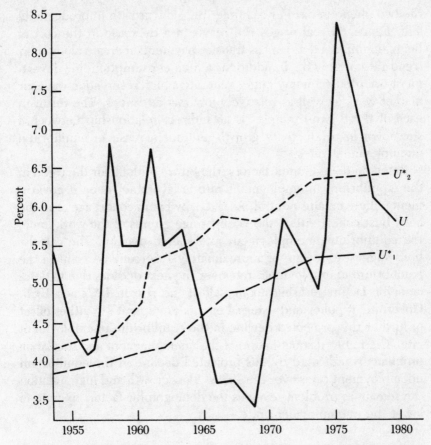

Figure 2-1 Estimating U, U^*_1, and U^*_2. (Source: Jeffrey M. Perloff and Michael L. Wachter, "*A Production Function Approach to Potential Output: Is Measured Potential Output Too High?*" Carnegie-Rochester Conference Series on Public Policy, *vol. 10, January 1979.*)

addition, the flattening of U^*_2 in the 1970s suggests that the food and fuel shocks and the slowdown in productivity have not had a further negative impact. While the stagflation problem largely emerged during the 1970s—and especially after 1973—the estimated increases in our U^* constructs were nearly completed prior to 1973.

The notion that the increase in U^* and the slowdown in productivity growth are independent of each other needs to be tempered by the difficulties in isolating the timing of these events. Moreover, economic theory does suggest important potential linkages between the two phenomena. For example, the slow growth in productivity and, hence, in real wages can result in a decrease in the cost of being unemployed as long as transfer payments increase along their trend rate of growth. In addition, a high consumption–low invest-ment-oriented economy might generate a high reservation wage for market work as well as relatively low market wages. The result in each of these two examples is an indirect relationship between a slowdown in productivity growth and an increase in equilibrium unemployment rates.

Based on demographic factors, the future outlook for the trend in the equilibrium unemployment rate is favorable, even if govern-ment policy remains neutral. As the baby boom cohort ages and the baby bust cohort enters the younger age groups of the work force, the equilibrium unemployment rate should decline. The calcula-tions suggest a decline of approximately 1 percentage point in the equilibrium unemployment rate over the next decade, due to dem-ographic factors' erasing about half of the rise in U^* since 1955. Government policy and external events can operate to either offset or further this projected decline in the equilibrium unemployment rate. The rather distinct nature of the unemployment and stagflation problems is indicated by this projected decline in the equilibrium unemployment rates over the 1980s. Slow growth and high inflation can remain as problems even as the demographic factors operate to lower the unemployment rate.

The Accelerating Inflation Rate

From a longer-run perspective, it appears that the increase in the inflation rate between 1965 and 1979 was due largely to overexpan-sionary monetary and fiscal policies. Exogenous shocks, such as the food and fuel price increases during the 1970s, can lead to ongoing inflation only if they are validated by aggregate demand policies. For example, although the large OPEC price increases in 1973–1974 and again in 1978–1979 may have caused a short-run increase in the inflation rate, the price level should have eventually settled at the new, higher level dictated by higher energy prices. If the in-creases in OPEC prices, however, lead to a higher rate of monetary growth and a large full-employment deficit, inflationary expecta-tions would have increased, the result being a short-run spike in the inflation rate which would become a long-run increase in the rate of inflation.

The Inflationary Bias of Government Policy

The inflationary bias of government policy can be seen by evaluating the GNP and unemployment targets of policymakers relative to attainable levels of potential GNP and equilibrium unemployment. The government's unemployment rate target has been consistently below the U^*_1 series. In the late 1960s the government target was 4 percent, while the equilibrium rate was between 4.9 and 5.4 percent. By the mid-1970s, when the government target was lifted to 4.9 percent, U^* had increased to between 5.5 and 6.0 percent. The systematic use by the monetary and fiscal authorities of an unemployment rate target below U^* has been a key ingredient in the increase in the inflation rate from an average of 1.5 percent in the early 1960s to the double digits of the early 1980s. Moreover, the "full-employment" budget surplus is seriously overstated by calculating that figure on the basis of a 5- or even 4-percent equilibrium, or full-employment, rate. The result is a tendency for fiscal policy to appear more restrictive than it actually is.

A lack of recognition of the effects of the demographic factors on the economy also seems apparent in the government's potential output for GNP target. Table 2–5 shows the measure of potential output that was used by the Council of Economic Advisers during the 1960s. According to that series, denoted *Old CEA*, potential output was always greater than actual output or GNP. More recently, the Council of Economic Advisers has reduced its measure of potential output. This new variable (denoted *New CEA*) is shown in column 4 of Table 2–5. Although actual GNP is occasionally above potential, this situation does not often occur. But if the economy always had economic slack, what explains the increase in the inflation rate over the past fifteen years?

The upper range, or optimistic estimate, of potential output, is denoted $QPOT_1$. This estimate, well below the government's current measure of potential, indicates that GNP was close to potential by the end of 1978. According to the lower range potential output estimate, the economy was overheating early in 1978. This pessimistic estimate of potential (denoted $QPOT_2$) differs from $QPOT_1$, in part, by using U^*_2 series and is provided along with $QPOT_1$ on a quarterly basis in Table 2–6.

Table 2–5   Alternative Measures of Potential Output (Billion 1972 Dollars)

Year	Actual GNP	Old CEA	New CEA	QPOT₁
1955	654.8	653.6	651.4	651.6
1956	668.8	676.6	673.9	670.8
1957	680.9	700.4	697.2	694.9
1958	679.5	725.0	721.3	722.5
1959	720.4	750.5	746.2	741.6
1960	736.8	776.9	771.9	767.0
1961	755.3	804.2	798.6	795.0
1962	799.1	832.5	826.4	821.0
1963	830.7	863.1	851.1	846.0
1964	874.4	895.6	890.3	874.2
1965	925.9	929.3	925.0	902.6
1966	981.0	964.3	960.8	944.1
1967	1007.7	1000.7	996.3	985.6
1968	1051.8	1038.4	1031.7	1017.6
1969	1078.8	1079.1	1068.3	1050.1
1970	1075.3	1122.5	1106.2	1085.1
1971	1107.5	1167.6	1145.5	1121.3
1972	1171.1	1214.6	1186.1	1157.1
1973	1235.0	1263.4	1227.0	1198.4
1974	1217.8	1314.2	1264.2	1234.7
1975	1202.3	1367.0	1302.1	1271.0
1976	1273.0	1422.0	1341.1	1316.8
1977	1340.5	1479.1	1381.4	1366.8
1978	1399.2	1538.6	1422.9	1404.8

SOURCES: The actual GNP and the Old and New Council of Economic Advisors potential output series are discussed in the Council of Economic Advisors report of 1979. The methodology for constructing $QPOT$ is presented in Jeffrey M. Perloff and Michael L. Wachter, "A Production Function-Nonaccelerating Inflation Approach to Potential Output: Is Measured Potential Output Too High?" *Carnegie-Rochester Conference Series on Public Policy*, K. Brunner and A. H. Meltzer, eds., vol. 10, 1979, pp. 113–163; and in "Reply," pp. 195–203.

Can Inflation Be Cured?

Given this view, what is the intermediate-run outlook for inflation and what are the costs of ongoing inflation? The outlook is impossible to predict because it rests largely upon the future decisions of the monetary and fiscal authorities.

One of the major problems in the anti-inflation battle is that the appropriate unemployment rate target for stabilization policy is not known with certainty. How far can the monetary and fiscal authorities push down the unemployment rate without accelerating inflation? In the 1960s, it was argued that uncertainty about the length of the lagged response of economic activity to aggregate demand

Table 2-6 Upper and Lower Ranges for Potential Output, Quarterly, 1955–
1978 (Billion 1972 Dollars)

Year	GNP	$QPOT_1$	$QPOT_2$
1955:01	641.10	636.68	641.97
1955:02	650.80	642.44	645.02
1955:03	660.30	650.02	653.37
1955:04	667.00	657.74	659.37
1956:01	664.10	663.81	662.05
1956:02	667.50	668.33	664.68
1956:03	667.90	676.42	671.85
1956:04	675.70	682.01	675.80
1957:01	680.40	688.96	683.22
1957:02	680.90	695.50	688.58
1957:03	685.60	701.23	696.08
1957:04	676.70	704.12	697.77
1958:01	663.40	710.21	703.10
1958:02	668.20	714.11	712.27
1958:03	684.40	722.37	723.18
1958:04	702.10	729.48	727.13
1959:01	710.70	734.17	727.78
1959:02	726.30	739.46	732.51
1959:03	718.60	740.74	734.68
1959:04	726.20	747.72	744.50
1960:01	740.70	756.89	751.96
1960:02	738.90	765.02	757.83
1960:03	735.70	770.39	762.16
1960:04	731.90	772.69	766.16
1961:01	736.60	781.31	777.27
1961:02	749.00	787.80	784.08
1961:03	758.70	793.97	790.21
1961:04	776.90	801.24	796.49
1962:01	788.10	809.54	805.79
1962:02	798.30	814.87	812.99
1962:03	804.30	819.46	816.31
1962:04	805.80	823.67	816.37
1963:01	813.50	832.87	826.05
1963:02	823.70	841.59	832.83
1963:03	838.80	847.65	843.41
1963:04	846.90	852.66	849.77
1964:01	861.10	861.42	860.38
1964:02	872.00	867.80	866.50
1964:03	880.50	875.37	869.95
1964:04	883.90	879.76	868.34
1965:01	903.00	891.32	881.43
1965:02	916.40	899.61	888.93
1965:03	932.30	908.48	901.61
1965:04	952.00	915.33	908.06

Table 2-6 (Continued)

Year	GNP	$QPOT_1$	$QPOT_2$
1966:01	969.60	929.37	924.06
1966:02	976.30	936.99	931.87
1966:03	985.40	946.91	941.35
1966:04	992.80	956.82	951.22
1967:01	994.40	969.87	965.49
1967:02	1001.3	977.11	972.45
1967:03	1013.6	990.11	987.08
1967:04	1021.5	996.55	990.64
1968:01	1031.4	1008.1	999.24
1968:02	1049.4	1014.9	1009.7
1968:03	1061.8	1026.1	1017.7
1968:04	1064.7	1028.5	1017.4
1969:01	1074.8	1043.4	1032.9
1969:02	1079.6	1054.0	1040.8
1969:03	1083.4	1062.2	1049.3
1969:04	1077.5	1067.5	1051.1
1970:01	1073.6	1080.1	1065.5
1970:02	1074.1	1088.6	1074.6
1970:03	1082.0	1094.5	1082.0
1970:04	1071.4	1103.8	1092.2
1971:01	1095.3	1116.7	1107.4
1971:02	1103.3	1122.7	1117.2
1971:03	1111.0	1128.2	1120.5
1971:04	1120.5	1121.7	1113.0
1972:01	1141.2	1149.9	1136.9
1972:02	1163.0	1155.8	1148.7
1972:03	1178.0	1158.2	1154.3
1972:04	1202.2	1165.4	1162.3
1973:01	1229.8	1181.4	1178.3
1973:02	1231.1	1190.2	1185.9
1973:03	1236.3	1197.7	1195.2
1973:04	1242.6	1211.5	1207.8
1974:01	1230.2	1212.7	1208.2
1974:02	1224.5	1233.1	1226.1
1974:03	1216.9	1244.4	1238.7
1974:04	1199.7	1240.4	1237.9
1975:01	1171.6	1256.0	1249.3
1975:02	1189.9	1265.4	1258.5
1975:03	1220.0	1279.0	1272.5
1975:04	1227.9	1283.6	1275.9
1976:01	1259.5	1299.4	1294.5
1976:02	1267.4	1306.2	1302.0
1976:03	1277.1	1322.9	1320.1

Table 2-6 (Continued)

Year	GNP	QPOT₁	QPOT₂
1976:04	1288.1	1325.1	1324.3
1977:01	1315.7	1341.6	1340.8
1977:02	1331.2	1357.6	1356.6
1977:03	1353.9	1371.0	1370.1
1977:04	1361.3	1379.3	1374.1
1978:01	1367.8	1379.9	1374.0
1978:02	1395.2	1400.2	1392.4
1978:03	1407.3	1414.0	1405.1
1978:04	1426.6	1429.3	1418.9

SOURCES: The actual GNP and the Old and New Council of Economic Advisors potential output series are discussed in the Council of Economic Advisors report of 1979. The methodology for constructing QPOT is presented in Jeffrey M. Perloff and Michael L. Wachter, "A Production Function-Nonaccelerating Inflation Approach to Potential Output: Is Measured Potential Output Too High?" *Carnegie-Rochester Conference Series on Public Policy*, K. Brunner and A. H. Meltzer, eds., vol. 10, 1979, pp. 113–163; and in "Reply," pp. 195–203.

policies was the key problem in fine tuning the economy. While that problem still exists, it is small compared with the issues raised by the uncertainty over the level of the sustainable unemployment rate. For example, this author's equilibrium unemployment estimates range between 5.5 and 6.2 percent.

In order to reduce the inflation rate, the evidence suggests the need for a longer-run commitment to avoid overheating the economy. Within this context, however, it is not necessary to restrict monetary and fiscal policy so as to encourage a recession. A more successful approach would be to focus on maintaining the unemployment rate at or near 6 percent, while slowly contracting the money supply growth rate. Several years would elapse before the inflation rate declined significantly as a result of such a policy, but the alternative seems grim—a continuation of accelerating inflation, combined with occasional recessions precipitated by abortive and short-lived attempts to reduce the inflation rate.

A key problem with using recessions to cure inflation is that they reduce the rate of capital accumulation and investment. The optimal monetary and fiscal policy to encourage maximum productivity and economic growth is a one that minimizes the variance in GNP growth rates. The adoption of this approach also requires using reasonable targets for potential output and equilibrium unemployment.

The Decline in Productivity

From 1948 to 1965, average productivity of labor, as measured by the Bureau of Labor Statistics, rose 2.7 percent per year. From 1968 to 1978, the rate of increase fell to 2.0 percent. Even more disturbing is the rate of decline since 1973. During 1973 and 1974, the decline was almost 5 percent; and since 1973 productivity growth has averaged about 1 percent per year.

Several hypotheses have been advanced to explain the decrease in the rate of productivity growth. Due to data limitations, only some of these explanations have been examined empirically. This section discusses the relationship between the cohort overcrowding hypothesis and the productivity slowdown; some preliminary empirical results are presented.

Demographic Factors

As long as the labor force is expanding in a manner that is largely unchanging over time, the demographic influences in productivity growth rates will be unimportant. The new entrants into the labor market and the unemployed are usually relatively young and un- skilled.

Recent demographic swings, however, suggest that the current cohort of new workers for the 1965-to-1980 period have had a differ- ent impact than the cohort that entered the labor market between 1950 and 1965. Even if both groups were of equal skill and educa- tion, the more recent cohort would have had a lower marginal product simply because the baby boom cohort was so large. With imperfect substitution between old and new workers, cohort over- crowding, as it occurred between 1965 and 1978, should have caused a decline in the productivity of new workers.

The shift from a relatively small to a large entering cohort low- ered the average productivity of the work force. As a conse- quence, the rate of change of productivity was reduced. These demo- graphic factors partially explain the large drop in productivity from 1950, when a small cohort of males entered the labor force, to the late 1970s, when a large cohort of young males and females entered.

The Marginal Productivity Series.   The Impact of demographic factors on the productivity slowdown is generally analyzed by using the traditional average productivity series. For productivity analysis, the more appropriate series is a marginal productivity series. However, this variable cannot be calculated from published data; rather, it must be calculated from an estimated production function. In this chapter, the marginal productivity series is calculated from the translog estimation that was used to calculate the potential output series $QPOT_1$ and $QPOT_2$. Since the translog production function used a labor input variable that weighted workers by their (fixed) relative wages, the resulting average and marginal productivities are adjusted for the changing age-sex composition of the labor force. The changes in the average product (ΔAPL) and marginal product (ΔMPL) series from 1956 to 1978 are shown in Table 2–7.

Table 2–7 Percentage Changes in Average and Marginal Products, Based on U^*_1

Year	Average Product (ΔAPL)	Marginal Product (ΔMPL)
1956	1.29	0.80
1957	2.51	2.37
1958	1.17	1.82
1959	4.23	3.88
1960	1.45	1.17
1961	2.27	1.93
1962	5.25	4.88
1963	3.45	3.09
1964	3.71	3.67
1965	4.53	4.78
1966	4.40	5.27
1967	2.02	2.28
1968	3.51	4.48
1969	1.46	2.17
1970	−0.12	−3.48
1971	2.59	0.82
1972	3.34	4.25
1973	2.60	4.41
1974	−2.52	−3.94
1975	1.17	−3.45
1976	2.90	3.87
1977	1.90	2.89
1978	0.73	2.61

SOURCES: The average productivity figures are based on government calculations. The marginal productivity series are derived in Jeffrey M. Perloff and Michael L. Wachter, "Alternative Approaches to Forecasting Potential Output, 1978–1980," *Proceedings of the American Statistical Association*, 1979, pp. 104–113; also, "A Production Function-Nonaccelerating Inflation Approach to Potential Output: Is Measured Potential Too High?" *Carnegie-Rochester Conference Series on Public Policy*, K. Brunner and A. H. Meltzer, eds., vol. 10, 1979, pp. 113–163, and "Reply," pp. 195–203.

Table 2-8   Productivity Growth Rates

Years	Unweighted Labor BLS (ΔAPL)	Percentage Changes in Average and Marginal Products	
		(ΔAPL)	(ΔMPL)
1956–1964	2.51	2.81	2.62
1965–1973	2.12	2.70	2.78
1974–1978	0.84	0.84	0.40

SOURCES: The average productivity figures are based on government calculations. The marginal productivity series are derived in Jeffrey M. Perloff and Michael L. Wachter, "Alternative Approaches to Forecasting Potential Output, 1978–1980," *Proceedings of the American Statistical Association*, 1979, pp. 104–113. Also, "A Production Function-Nonaccelerating Inflation Approach to Potential Output: Is Measured Potential Too High?" *Carnegie-Rochester Conference Series on Public Policy*, K. Brunner and A. H. Meltzer, eds., vol. 10, 1979. pp. 113–163, and "Reply," pp. 195–203.

In Table 2–8, the data for the 1956–1978 period are divided into the following subperiods: 1960–1964, 1965–1973, and 1974–1978. The most striking finding after the data are adjusted for the age and sex demographic changes is that the rate of change of marginal productivity actually increases between the 1956–1964 and 1965–1973 periods. The demographic-adjusted marginal productivity series increased at a 2.62 percent rate in the earlier period, compared to a 2.78 percent rate in the later period. This positive differential growth rate between periods of 0.16 percent compares with a negative 0.4 percent differential in the unweighted series. Hence, the swing due to the demographic adjustment is more than half a percent, or 0.56 percent.

The Significance of Choice of Years.   This type of subperiod analysis, however, can be misleading. The data in Tables 2–7 and 2–8 indicate the importance of the choice of years in dividing the total period. For example, the years 1965 and 1966 have two of the three largest productivity gains over the past twenty-five years. Hence, changing the dating of the middle period from 1965–1973 to 1967–1973 makes a significant difference in the results. The overall marginal productivity growth rate for the period 1967–1973 is only 2.13 percent, which is down from 3 percent for the period 1956–1966. The unexpected productivity speedup thus becomes a more traditional slowdown.

It is, however, reasonable to start this period in 1965. Besides corresponding to a point in the business cycle where U is approximately equal to U^*, which is also true of 1956 and 1973, the year 1965 corresponds to a point in the demographic cycle when the first baby boom cohort entered the labor force in large numbers. (The oldest members of the baby boom cohort began to enter the labor market around 1960.)

The Inadequacy of Demographic Adjustment. Although a demographic adjustment for age and sex can explain the decline in productivity between 1965 and the early 1970s, this adjustment does not explain the major slowdown that began during the early 1970s. Indeed, the success of the demographic explanation in the early period, compared with its lack of success in the latest period, implies that an even more pronounced slowdown occurred after the early 1970s than is shown by an adjusted productivity series. In other words, adjusting the labor input series for age and sex compositional shifts alters the timing, but not the size, of the productivity slowdown. The onset of any significant slowdown appears to be delayed until the early 1970s. The result is to change a gradual slowdown into a dramatic collapse of the productivity growth rate. As seen in Table 2–8, the ΔMPL series increases at a 2.62 percent rate from 1956 to 1964, and at a 2.78 percent rate from 1965 to 1973; but it grows at only a 0.40 percent rate from 1974 to 1978.

The Shortfall in Capital Expenditures

Several explanations have been offered for the slowdown in productivity in the early 1970s. Perhaps the most widely held view is that a shortfall in capital expenditures contributed to the productivity decline by reducing the trend growth in the capital-labor ratio. This conclusion arises most strongly in studies that use the growth accounting approach. Such studies, however, do not really explain the slowdown. Rather, they attribute that portion of the slowdown that parallels changes in input growth rates to the various inputs. As a result, the reduction in the growth of capital-labor ratios is viewed as the explanatory factor because both output and capital-labor ratios follow similar time paths between 1973 and 1979.

Although some economists argue that a falloff in capital expenditures is the cause of the productivity slowdown, the techniques used to determine the fact that capital-labor ratios are growing more slowly than in earlier years are compatible—in a general equilibrium context—with either capital growing "too slowly" or labor growing "too fast."

Research on the investment function has isolated several factors that might account for the investment slowdown. For example, papers presented throughout the series of Special Studies on Economic Change by the Joint Economic Committee consistently highlight two major factors as causes: (1) Increases in the acceptable or hurdle rate of return on new investments due to the additional uncertainty generated by the inflation, and (2) effects of the deep recession of 1974–1975. In the translog production function approach, the slowdown in productivity can be attributed to (1) capital, labor, and energy growth patterns; (2) Hicks neutral technological change; and (3) cyclical factors. Although an investigation of these various factors is beyond the scope of this paper, our focus on the stagflation question makes it particularly relevant to explore the influence of the 1974–1975 recession on the productivity slowdown.

The Potential Marginal Productivity Series

Since our potential output series are calculated on the assumption that the economy has an unemployment rate equal to its equilibrium rate, the *potential* average and marginal productivity series (denoted ΔAPL^* and ΔMPL^*, respectively) yield a *cyclically corrected* productivity series. These series are presented in Table 2–9. The labor inputs in both the ΔAPL^* and ΔMPL^* series are adjusted for demographic as well as cyclical factors.

A comparison of the ΔMPL and ΔMPL^* series in Tables 2–7 and 2–9 yields several striking results. First, if only a demographic correction is made (ΔMPL), productivity growth actually increases between the 1956–1964 and 1965–1973 periods. However, if both demographic and cyclical adjustments (ΔMPL^*) based on U^* are made, productivity appears to decrease slightly. As indicated in Table 2–10, the ΔMPL^* series averages 2.81 percent during the 1955–1964 period and then slows to 2.47 percent in the 1965–1973 period.

Second, the ΔMPL^* series is useful for analyzing turning points in the productivity growth rate. The timing of the productivity slowdown has been a focal point of the current debate. The recent years have been broken into numerous subdivisions in an attempt to isolate the onset of the recent slowdown. For example, the view that the increase in energy prices has been the major causal factor would require that the significant decrease in productivity growth occurred after 1973. While the post–1973 ΔAPL^* and ΔMPL^* figures are below historical averages, these series peaked in 1965 or

Table 2–9 Percentage Changes in Potential Average and Marginal Products, Based on U^*_1

Year	Potential Average Product (ΔAPL^*)	Potential Marginal Product (ΔMPL^*)
1956	3.51	3.39
1957	3.33	3.15
1958	2.73	2.56
1959	2.85	2.87
1960	2.80	2.71
1961	2.71	2.57
1962	2.73	2.65
1963	2.79	2.68
1964	2.78	2.71
1965	3.05	2.95
1966	3.43	3.23
1967	3.24	3.01
1968	2.85	2.73
1969	2.77	2.85
1970	2.50	2.30
1971	1.63	1.54
1972	1.98	1.98
1973	1.87	1.86
1974	1.45	1.36
1975	1.08	0.89
1976	1.41	1.45
1977	1.40	1.43
1978	0.63	0.74

SOURCES: The average productivity figures are based on government calculations. The marginal productivity series are derived in Jeffrey M. Perloff and Michael L. Wachter, "Alternative Approaches to Forecasting Potential Output, 1978–1980," *Proceedings of the American Statistical Association*, 1979, pp. 104–113. Also, "A Production Function-Nonaccelerating Inflation Approach to Potential Output: Is Measured Potential Too High?" *Carnegie-Rochester Conference Series on Public Policy*, K. Brunner and A. H. Meltzer, eds., vol. 10, 1979, pp. 113–163, and "Reply," pp. 195–203.

1966 and decreased thereafter. Substantial drops occurred in 1971 and in other years. Thus, other factors besides just energy must affect productivity.

Third, the cyclical adjustment correction results in a threefold increase in the productivity growth rate in the 1974–1978 period. While ΔMPL between 1974 and 1978 grows at 0.40 percent (see Table 2–7), ΔMPL^* grows at 1.17 percent over the same period. (see Table 2–10). Moreover, the ΔMPL^* series growth rate is also higher than the rate calculated by the Bureau of Labor Statistics' Q/L (average productivity) series. Although the cyclical correction

Table 2-10   Percentage Changes in Potential Average and Marginal Products

Years	(Based on U*$_1$)		(Based on U*$_2$)	
	ΔAPL*	ΔMPL*	ΔAPL*	ΔMPL
1956–1964	2.91	2.81	2.81	2.29
1965–1973	2.59	2.47	2.60	2.33
1974–1978	1.19	1.17	1.24	1.20

SOURCES: The average productivity figures are based on government calculations. The marginal productivity series are derived in Jeffrey M. Perloff and Michael L. Wachter, "Alternative Approaches to Forecasting Potential Output, 1978–1980." *Proceedings of the American Statistical Association,* 1979, pp. 104–113. Also, "A Production Function-Nonaccelerating Inflation Approach to Potential Output: Is Measured Potential Too High?" *Carnegie-Rochester Conference Series on Public Policy,* K. Brunner and A. H. Meltzer, eds., vol. 10, 1979, pp. 113–163, and "Reply," pp. 195–203.

yields a significant upward revision of the productivity growth rate, 1.17 percent is still a very low productivity growth rate by historical standards.

Indeed, a case could be made for the major drop having started in 1970 or 1971. Such a view would not only be consistent with misallocations created by the Nixon price controls program but also in line with expansion of government regulatory programs—both contributors to the productivity decline.

Productivity Developments for Different Industry Sectors

It would be useful to test the above findings by adjusting disaggregated data by major industry classifications for demographic and cyclical variations. Unfortunately, reliable age-sex employment data by industry have only been available since 1967. The unadjusted average productivity changes for the eight major industries are shown in Table 2–11.

Productivity Patterns by Industry

Although the unweighted aggregate productivity measure declines significantly between the periods 1948–1964 and 1965–1973, the patterns for major industry groups differ greatly. A pronounced productivity decline is evident only in those industries for which the data are least reliable or where special factors would be relevant— for example, mining; construction; and finance, insurance, and real

Table 2-11   Average Productivity Growth Rates in Which Labor Is *Not* Weighted for Demographic Changes (in Percent)

| | | | | | | Major Industry Groups | | | |
| | | | | | | | Retail and | | |
Years	Aggregate	Mining	Construction	Nondurables	Durables	Transportation	Wholesale Trade	FIRE	Service
1948–1964	2.46	4.34	2.11	3.41	2.38	3.68	2.44	1.61	0.04
1965–1973	1.72	1.71	−2.12	2.78	2.23	3.98	2.11	0.41	0.62
1974–1978	0.92	−5.25	−0.95	3.20	0.92	1.91	0.26	1.85	−0.83

SOURCE: Unpublished numbers provided by the Department of Commerce.

Table 2-12   Average Productivity Growth Rates in Which Labor Is Weighted for Demographic Changes, ΔAPL (in Percent)

| | | | | | | Major Industry Groups | | | |
| | | | | | | | Retail and | | |
Years	Aggregate	Mining	Construction	Nondurables	Durables	Transportation	Wholesale Trade	FIRE	Services
1967–1973	1.91	−0.21	−2.29	4.34	3.10	3.74	2.65	0.27	−0.26
1974–1978	1.17	−3.54	−0.09	3.35	0.89	1.07	1.52	1.34	−0.31

Table 2-13   Average Productivity Growth Rates in Which Labor Is Weighted for Demographic Changes and Cyclically Adjusted, ΔAPL^*, Based on U^*_1 (in Percent)

| | | | | | | Major Industry Groups | | | |
| | | | | | | | Retail and | | |
Years	Aggregate	Mining	Construction	Nondurables	Durables	Transportation	Wholesale Trade	FIRE	Services
1967–1973	2.13	−0.62	−3.51	4.46	3.70	3.09	3.00	0.38	0.83
1974–1978	1.70	−4.10	−0.63	3.34	2.43	1.87	2.14	1.47	0.12

estate (FIRE). The productivity decline in mining may be due to the adoption of health and safety regulations or output shifts within the mining sector. The output data in construction and FIRE are very unreliable. Where the data are most reliable—in the durables and retail and wholesale trade industries—the productivity growth rate is relatively constant between these two periods. Stability is also evident in transportation and services. Although these latter data series also have problems, they are not as severe as the problems in construction and FIRE.

The calculations shown in Table 2–11 suggest that, in addition to the demographic effects stressed above, data problems and industry-specific developments (largely in mining) are factors in the aggregate productivity decline. This reasoning is consistent with the view that the productivity component of the stagflation problem was not present prior to the 1970s. Although aggregate productivity appears to be declining in this earlier period, much of the decline could be traced to the same demographic factors that were causing the increase in the equilibrium unemployment rate. In other words, compositional shifts and cohort overcrowding were causing biases in the published productivity and unemployment rate data.

Analyzing Productivity Trends

An analysis of productivity trends in the major industry categories is also useful in confirming that a "true" productivity decline occurred during the 1970s. The unadjusted series are presented in Table 2–11 for the periods 1948–1964, 1965–1973, and 1974–1978. The adjusted series for 1967–1973 and 1974–1978 are shown in Table 2–12. As previously indicated, the productivity slowdown appears to be larger after the effect of the demographic compositional shifts is incorporated into the data. The demographic adjustment causes the productivity growth rate for the 1967–1973 period to be revised upward substantially, while leaving the rate for the 1974–1978 period virtually unchanged. Thus, the revised series shows a more pronounced slowdown than the unrevised data. Indeed, the demographically adjusted productivity series shows large declines between 1967–1973 and 1974–1978 in all major industries except construction and FIRE—the two industries where the data are least reliable.

Finally, Tables 2–12 and 2–13 that ΔAPL and ΔAPL^* differ substantially across industries. Of particular interest are those industries for which we have reliable data. In durables manufacturing, transportation, and trade, the cyclically corrected series (ΔAPL^*) shows a smaller slowdown. For example, in durables, ΔAPL in the 1967–1973 period was 3.10 percent and in 1974–1978 was 0.89 percent, which yields a difference between these figures of 2.21 percentage points. The comparable figures for ΔAPL^* are 3.70, 2.43, and 1.27 percentage points. That is, the cyclically adjusted series slows by 1 percent less than the unadjusted series. The nondurables series shows a slight, but not statistically significant, increase for the cyclically adjusted series.

Implications for the 1980s

In addition to being an important determinant of today's economic problems, the changing demographic composition of the population and labor force will also have a crucial role in economic developments over the next decade. To an important extent, these developments will represent an unwinding of the supply-side bottlenecks caused by the baby boom or cohort overcrowding.

The Dwindling Number of New Entrants into the Labor Force

Overall labor force growth, having increased significantly during the past decade to approximately 2.5 million new workers per year, has peaked. On the basis of the cohort overcrowding model, the number of new workers is predicted to decline to approximately 1.5 million new workers per year by the late 1980s.

The dwindling number of new entrants will coincide with an aging of the labor force. Labor force participation rates of older workers will again begin to increase relative to the participation rates of younger people. The result, especially compared with the current period, will be a shortage of younger, less-skilled workers relative to older workers with more specific training. This shift in the composition of the labor force should result in a noticeable decline in the equilibrium unemployment rate (U^*). The decline, which should begin around 1981, will become most pronounced after 1985.

Changes in Female and Youth Participation Rates

An important question is whether the effects of the aging of the population will be offset by changes in participation rates, especially by young female groups. The evidence suggests that this will not occur, a prediction based on the cohort overcrowding model and the underlying trends in the age structure of the population.

What is most likely to happen is that the past decade's increase in young female participation rates will begin to spill over into higher participation rates for older females. As they grow older, the young females of the 1970s will continue to have higher participation rates than their predecessors. The shift from increasing participation rates for younger to older females will have beneficial effects on the equilibrium unemployment rate for the overall economy for this reason: Females age 35 and over have equilibrium unemployment rates that are close to those of prime-age males and are considerably below those of younger females.

For youth aged 16 to 24, the outlook for future changes in participation rates is mixed. Changes in these rates mirror closely the changes in school enrollment and fertility rates. Although over the past few decades school enrollment rates have been declining for males age 16 to 19 and have remained steady for males age 20 to 24, these negative trends have most likely been a reflection of cohort overcrowding effects. As the baby bust cohort replaces the baby boom cohort in the 16- to 24-year-old group and the life-cycle income prospects for youth increases, school enrollment rates are likely to resume their historical upward trend. For young females, school enrollment rates have continued to increase over the past decade, and the prospects for the future are for an even greater increase in female enrollment rates. The effects of the cohort overcrowding model are also likely to translate into slowly rising fertility rates over the 1980s and this rise will tend to dampen participation-rate increases for females below the age of 35.

The only element that argues for higher youth participation rates is the trend toward part-time work. This development has been noted for both school-age youth and females with very young children. Since an individual is counted as being in the labor force as long as he or she is working or even looking for a part-time job, the figures on participation rates are biased upward. This author's view is that although the tendency for school enrollees and very young workers to work part-time will not decrease, it should stabilize near current levels. Today's younger workers were born near the end of the baby boom—that is, they are generally the last child (perhaps third or fourth child) in the larger baby boom families. Through high school and college years, they have felt strong family and financial pressures to work part of the time. These pressures are likely to subside rapidly as the children from smaller families reach the 16- to 24-year-old age groups.

Changes in Hours Worked

Another potential factor affecting the growth rate of the labor supply is the change in hours worked. The available supply of workers in the future could be significantly altered by a decrease in the number of hours worked per individual. Certainly, a major policy issue today is whether workers will make the issue of a shorter workweek an important part of their collective bargaining posture. There is some evidence that the long secular decline in hours worked per week virtually stopped after World War II. (See Chapter Five.) Although data problems make it difficult to discuss this possibility with the desired precision, it is clear that any decline in hours worked after 1947 has been relatively small compared with the downward trend prior to World War II.

The Baby Boom Cohort. Is the apparent stability in hours worked per week likely to continue into the near- and intermediate-term future? To date, this author's investigations suggest a strong likelihood that such stability will continue. An important factor in this forecast involves the poor labor market performance of the baby boom group that resulted from the cohort overcrowding effect. As this group ages and enters its prime working years, it is less likely to opt for early retirement or for fewer hours of work. Traditionally, a reduction in hours of work has been part of a trade-off in which the higher standard of living obtainable by society has been divided into a higher standard of living and additional hours of leisure, or reduced work—that is, society, rather than choosing maximum output and maximum work, takes part of the growth dividend in increased leisure. Over the next several years, slow productivity growth will reduce the size of the bonus that can be translated into a reduction in hours. Given the importance of achieving desired living standards, it is unlikely that the low bonus associated with the low productivity growth of the coming years will lead people to seek shorter hours. Moreover, the cohort overcrowding phenomena itself puts limits on the standard-of-living improvements available to the baby boom generation as it ages.

The Baby Bust Cohort.   Of some interest is whether or not the baby bust cohort will be a factor favoring shorter workweeks. To the extent that this group benefits from higher relative income—given its aspiration levels—it may opt for fewer hours. However, potential countervailing factors exist here. First is the high fixed cost associated with training for many occupations. Since the baby bust cohort is a better-educated group relative to the baby boom cohort, it may not be willing to amortize its training costs over fewer hours of work. Second, and perhaps more important, is the racial composition of the baby bust cohort, which will be quite different from the racial composition of the baby boom cohort. The baby bust group will contain a much higher percentage of minority workers than did the baby boom generation. These minority workers, given the possibility of higher income and greater upward mobility, may opt for the current level of work hours in order to improve their position relative to nondisadvantaged workers. Because aspiration levels are based on intersocioeconomic as well as intercohort comparisons, there will be important pressures on some members of the baby bust group against taking advantage of the higher relative income (defined across cohorts) to achieve additional leisure.

Part-Time Workers.   Underlining the various elements that support reduction in hours worked is the fact that 25 percent of the current part-time workers are "moonlighters"—that is, many workers who now face "shorter hours on the job" make up for these shorter hours by simply working a second job. In other words, one must differentiate between the number of hours worked in a given industry and the individual worker's interest in working a given number of hours. Labor union pressures toward obtaining shorter hours of work may continue to the extent that these shorter hours can be achieved without reducing take-home pay and, perhaps more important, retirement benefits. But workers will continue to be unwilling to take fewer hours of work if their retirement and take-home incomes are adjusted for the hours reduction.

Prospects for the Baby Boom Cohort

Although our cohort overcrowding model and the discussion in the preceding sections are basically inverted to study the slowing of population growth, this is not uniformly the case. In particular, as the baby bust cohort replaces the baby boom cohort in the labor market, the shortage input will be entry-level workers drawn from the dwindling supply of new entrants. However, a relative decline in the number of young or experienced workers is easier for the economy to adjust to than is a scarcity of more experienced or skilled workers. Experienced workers can be downgraded quickly to fill jobs requiring less skills, but young, inexperienced workers cannot be upgraded as rapidly to fill higher-level positions.

In this new environment, then, the labor market problem will shift from integrating a young population into the work force to adjusting to the continual problems of the now older baby boom workers, who are consigned to ongoing competition within a relatively large cohort group. Promotion opportunities for this older group will be unfavorable, and the less successful, or lower-attachment workers, may well remain in the traditional entry-level positions to compensate for the scarcity of new entrants.

Although the unemployment rate of the baby boom cohort should decline as the cohort ages, its *relative* wage or income experience will likely remain somewhat unfavorable. The problem for this group will switch from unemployment to low wages. In this environment the emphasis of macroeconomic government policy should remain on supply-side issues, such as human and physical capital accumulation, which can translate into a higher rate of growth of productivity and real wages.

Perhaps the final economic burden for the baby boom cohort will involve their retirement years. The Social Security system (OASDI) is currently paying high benefits to retirees, but the benefits are being financed by the baby boom generation rather than by the recipients. When the baby boom generation approaches retirement, however, and if current replacement levels are maintained in the workforce, the number of people who will be able to support the retiring workers will be too low. Similar problems exist for the disability and health benefits of the OASDI program. Hence, the baby boom generation faces a shortfall in OASDI benefits relative to its expectations as well as a shortfall in current income.

The difficulties in paying retirement benefits to a burgeoning population of senior citizens, coupled with the unfavorable labor market experiences of the baby boom generation, may result in some slowdown or even reversal in the future average retirement age—a result that could serve as a safety valve for some of the problems that will arise from the demographic twist.

Demographic Developments Outside the United States

In analyzing the implications of the demographic twist, it must be stressed that the second half of the twist—namely, the population growth slowdown—has occurred largely in the United States and Europe but not in most less developed countries. Where national economies are increasingly linked together through international trade and "temporary" migration of workers, the impact of domestic population changes in the United States may be offset by demographic developments elsewhere. For example, although the demographic twist may contribute to a slowdown in the growth rate of U.S. demand for food and fuel, increases in international population and development are likely to maintain an increased international demand for these items. Bottlenecks associated with food and fuel may therefore be a recurring event that will result in unanticipated, and perhaps sharp, upswings in the equilibrium unemployment rate and the domestic rate of inflation.

The Role of Macroeconomic Policy

In order to determine what policies should be used to lower the inflation and unemployment rates and increase the rate of productivity growth, one must be knowledgeable of the factors responsible for the problems. Although increasing inflation and unemployment and decreasing productivity growth have similar roots, they also have distinctive qualities.

Policies Affecting Unemployment

If cyclical unemployment were a significant component of the overall unemployment rate, then monetary and fiscal policies could be used to decrease the unemployment rate and increase population. This chapter has maintained that much of the increase in the unemployment rate over the past two to three decades can be traced to the changing composition of the labor force. It is largely the cohort overcrowding that caused the equilibrium unemployment rate to increase from approximately 4 percent in the mid-1950s to approximately 6 percent in 1980. Since most of the increase in the unemployment rate reflects an increase in the equilibrium unemployment rate, countercyclical monetary and fiscal policies cannot lower unemployment, except at the cost of accelerating inflation. Other policies, however, including job training and employment tax credits, could be used to lower the equilibrium unemployment rate.

It should be recognized, though, that these other policies, even if successful, will have only a negligible effect on productivity growth. The workers who are part of the unemployment pool at U^* are low-wage workers with limited skills. Improving the skills and, hence, the employability and market wages of these workers could be extremely beneficial to the workers themselves and to society. But, because of their low skills, moving these workers from being unemployed to employed will have little impact on the level of production and productivity. (Actually, the average product series generally used in the published data would probably decline because of the additional compositional shift toward low-wage workers.) Thus we have a trade-off between those programs that have their major impact on U^* and those that have their greatest impact on productivity growth.

As mentioned previously, the intermediate-term outlook for unemployment is favorable, even if government policy is hereafter neutral. As the baby boom cohort ages and the baby bust cohort enters into younger age groups within the workforce, the equilibrium unemployment rate will decline. This author suggests a decline of approximately 1 percent in the equilibrium unemployment rate over the next decade. This gain will be due solely to the demographic factor. Government policy and external events can operate to either offset or further this projected decline in the equilibrium unemployment rate.

Policies Affecting Productivity Growth

The major element in the stagflation picture is the slowdown in real economic growth. The current inflation and unemployment rates would be considerably less painful if the rate of real economic growth were to increase. At present, the rate of growth of potential output (using POT_1 and POT_2) is approximately 3 percent. After adjusting for the growth in the labor force, we are left with a dismal record in per capita terms.

The general shape of policies to increase real GNP growth rates are well known. The basic requirement is to shift away from policies that encourage consumption and move toward those that encourage investment. This approach would require a major overhaul in the tax structure as well as a change in priorities for government expenditure programs. Contrary to conventional wisdom, such policies need not increase the gap between high- and low-income families. Incentives for increased savings rates can be targeted at the middle class, and government expenditure programs can be aimed at increasing the "human capital" of our lowest skilled workers. Obviously, describing the details of a high growth rate policy is beyond the scope of this chapter.

Finally, the evidence presented here indicates that some of the slowdown in productivity has been due to the unusually large cyclical fluctuations that took place in the economy in the 1970s. Therefore, monetary and fiscal policies should be adopted to reduce the variance of output and unemployment. The increased uncertainty generated by the cyclical swings is a potentially important factor in retarding productivity growth. Although the government's official policy is to dampen the business cycle, it is this author's belief that by adopting unrealistic unemployment and potential output targets, the monetary and fiscal authorities may have intensified underlying swings in the economy over the recent past.

The Impact of Immigration

One way of forecasting the potential role of immigration in the U.S. labor market of the 1980s is to compare labor supply and demand projections for that period. The "cohort overcrowding model," described previously, provides a labor forecast that focuses on the likely impact of the demographic twist over the next decade. The demographic twist is the changeover in the younger age groups from the oversized baby boom cohort to the undersized baby bust cohort—that is, the cohort born during the very low fertility rates of the late 1960s and 1970s. This important development on the *supply side* of the labor market is compared with the Bureau of Labor Statistics' *demand-side* projections for occupational employment up to 1985. The BLS study foresees continuation of the gradual shift from blue-collar employment toward white-collar and service work.

The comparison permits identification of those occupations and age-sex groups that are likely to have a decline of workers and matches the characteristics of the shortage categories with the demographic characteristics of the illegal alien work force. For expositional purposes and because of a lack of data, the projections assume that the age-sex requirements of occupations remain unchanged from their 1970 levels. This approach highlights those occupations where the demand and labor supply models diverge.

Where the two models diverge, the projected gap can be filled in several ways. Left alone, the market mechanism would be expected to alter the relative prices and wages of different skill groups and capital so as to reduce the supply and demand gap. If the discrepancies are relatively large, the necessary changes in relative wages and prices may also be large, and lags in adjustments may result in a prolonged period in which relative unemployment rates change as well. Over time, however, the workings of the market should ensure equality between occupational supply and demand.

Legalizing and Controlling the Flow of Immigrants

To the extent that the relative wage and unemployment adjustments are politically painful, society may seek other modes of adjustment. Legalizing and controlling the total flow of immigrants is one such method. Increased immigration, however, is only useful if the projected gaps are for lower-skilled workers. In fact, the projections do suggest a likely shortfall of lower-skilled male workers in the 1985–1990 period. This projection is largely a function of the supply changes resulting from the movement from the baby boom cohort to the baby bust cohort in the younger working age group.

The clear message of the labor supply and demand projections is that illegal aliens will be in even greater demand in the United States in the 1980s than they are today. The normal growth of the economy will have a tendency to pull in additional illegal immigrants so as to maintain an approximately constant relationship with the overall growth of the labor force. More importantly, the replacement of the baby boom cohort with the baby bust cohort in entry-level positions creates additional pressures for an increase in the number of illegal aliens. Assuming an illegal alien work force of 4.87 million in 1977, a conservative estimate of the potential growth factor for illegal aliens may be approximately 65 percent by 1990. That projection would imply over 8 million illegal alien workers. If the assumption that there were 4.9 million illegal alien workers in 1977 is incorrect, then the 1990 number would also be incorrect by roughly the same percentage.

Immigration Policies and Their Effect on the Labor Force

In assessing the implications of the labor market projections for illegal immigration, several issues need to be raised. First, could the United States stop the influx of illegal immigrants if, *ceteris paribus*, that were the desired policy option? Second, what groups of American individuals would be aided and what groups harmed by moving toward a more open or flexible immigration policy? And what would be the effect of such policies on firms? Third, what type of immigration policy would maximize the gains and minimize the costs to American citizens?

This study suggests the following conclusions. Since it would be almost impossible to seal the borders of the United States, illegal immigration can probably only be stopped by a combination of workers' identification cards and monetary penalties against firms that hire workers who lack such cards. But maintaining and even increasing the flow of immigrants could have benefits as well as costs. The impact does not depend on whether the immigration is legal or illegal, but rather on the demographic characteristic of the immigrants. A critical assumption of this analysis is that these immigrants would be predominantly unskilled.

In the 1980s as the rate of increase in the native labor force declines, an increased flow of immigrants would benefit skilled older workers and the owners of capital. More specifically it would benefit the baby boom cohort as that group enters the 30-and-over age categories in the 1980s. Increased immigration would allow an increase in relative income levels and occupational attainment of that cohort. These potential gains compare with a further decline in the baby boom cohort's position if immigration flows are actually reduced in the 1980s.

Whereas skilled workers would benefit from an increased flow of immigrants, unskilled workers would be likely to face reduced relative incomes and higher unemployment rates. This economic trade-off between illegal immigrants and the unskilled, especially the disadvantaged, work force seems unavoidable.

The magnitude of the gains and losses in the late 1980s, however, will differ from those of the late 1970s. Essentially the gains will be greater and the losses will be smaller because there will be fewer unskilled, younger domestic workers and many more older and skilled workers. On the other hand, the domestic unskilled labor supply will be increasingly dominated by minority workers. In the 1980s the trade-off between accepting more immigrant workers and improving the economic position of the domestic disadvantaged population is likely to become a critical public policy issue.

The major conclusion of this chapter regarding immigration policy is that the current lack of clearly articulated and enforced policy will have to be changed. The unprecedented changes in the demographic structure of the labor force will create the need for a new enforceable policy. The exact parameters of that policy will be determined in the political arena. From a purely economic viewpoint, however, there are many advantages to a kind of "guest-worker" policy, where immigrants are granted work permits that do not imply permanent permission to remain in this country. The system has greater flexibility than alternative policy options in adjusting the stock of guest workers in either direction. This advantage is particularly important for monitoring the effects of the system on the relative economic gains of disadvantaged, unskilled native workers.

The guest-worker approach raises important social and political issues. Economic considerations alone will probably not dictate what policy is selected. Ultimately, the immigration policy that will be adopted will be decided through a political process. Still, the economic pressures existing from the demographic twist in this country, and the continued low wage and high population growth in some neighboring countries, do suggest that the United States can no longer ignore the immigration question.

Chapter 3

EARLY RETIREMENT: BOON OR BANE?

by Eli Ginzberg

Retirement is a relatively new social phenomenon. Pensions were unknown in the past except perhaps to a favored few who, like Dr. Johnson, drew a pension from the Crown but never stopped working. Today we have mandatory retirement, which forces some workers out of the labor market sooner than they would like. On the other hand, we have a relatively new twist to the retirement picture, in that some workers now want to retire early. This chapter, through the use of a survey of early retirees, explores some of the whys and wherefores of early retirement and what this trend implies for current and future policies at both the corporate and public levels.

The Need to Investigate the Issues of Early Retirement

A generation ago, the norm for retirement was age 65. The Social Security Act gave powerful sanction to this retirement age, and the large numbers of private pension plans that developed since then usually accepted age 65 as a norm. In addition, many large corporations began to set 65 as the age of mandatory retirement, even if exceptions were often made. In spite of these powerful institutional rules, a steady erosion of that norm has taken place. The labor force participation rates of older age groups have shown a steady, and recently quite rapid, decline since the 1950s. In some well-publicized instances, prominent corporations have developed plans to induce the early retirement of certain segments of their labor

77

force, particularly engineers. In other instances less publicized and more indirect (even covert) pressures have been exerted to induce selected individuals to retire early.

Because of the nature of the managerial pyramid and the possible obsolescence of professional and technical skills, early retirement of middle-level managerial and professional/technical personnel has, in some cases, seemed to offer a solution to such troubling problems as career plateaus, blockage of promotions, and technological lags.

From the point of view of the employee, early retirement has become more tempting. Generous pension offers, very large accumulations of assets, and long tenure with a company (so that an individual can say to himself, "I have worked long enough, paid my dues"), combined with the new phenomenon of the two-worker family, have fueled the trend toward early retirement.

The following questions related to actual or potential policy issues of corporations or the public at large provide, in part, the framework and purpose for our investigation into early retirement.

1. If early retirement has become more common, what will be its effects on the manpower planning of large corporations, on pension plans, and on other employee benefit plans?

2. What will be the effect of changes in the law raising the legal age for mandatory retirement to 70?

3. What will be the potential effects of the Age Discrimination in Employment Act?

4. Do managerial employees who have often spent many decades of loyal and productive service with a large corporation elect early retirement because the grass is really greener outside, or because the corporation has allowed its own pastures to seem (or be) very brown for many middle-level managers and professional/technical employees?

5. Do highly educated, experienced, productive individuals who retire when they are still vigorous represent an important underutilized resource that neither the nation nor they themselves can really afford to waste?

6. Have plans to retire early been frustrated by unanticipated inflation?

7. Have some early retirees found ways to reenter the private sector or found significant and satisfying roles in the public sector or in nonprofit services?

8. What lessons can be distilled from the experiences of early retirees that might help others understand the opportunities and challenges of early retirement?

Who Was Surveyed?

A total of 1,045 persons filled out the retirement questionnaire. The participating companies drew a structured sample, which was developed by the investigators, to ensure a reasonable distribution among persons who had left employment within the last ten years. Persons were included in the sample if, on the basis of 1978 dollars, they earned not less than $20,000 on retirement and not more than $50,000. The following list provides a profile of the respondents:

1. Most retired before their sixty-third birthday, after an average of thirty-six years with their employer.
2. Over half worked thirty-six years or more with their company; only one in ten for less than twenty-five years.
3. Most were males, and most were married at the time of their response.
4. Over half did not have a college degree.
5. Most served in a managerial position before retirement.
6. Most who continued working did so in a professional or technical capacity.

The Retirement Decision

The decision to make a lifestyle change as dramatic as retirement can't be an easy one. It affects a person's social life, personal life, and especially one's financial situation.

Unelected Retirement

Not all of the respondents in the survey had the option to continue working, however. About 30 percent had been forced out of their job in some manner or encouraged to leave. Changes in management, reductions in personnel or interpersonal conflicts with superiors made early retirement the most comfortable option in an untenable work situation. One respondent in such a position wrote: "I had not planned early retirement, as my job was exciting, challenging, and management at that point in time was excellent. However—a complete change in management occurred in 1975." An additional 25 percent of the respondents reached mandatory age (something less than 65 years old) for their level in the company and had no choice but to retire.

Elected Retirement

The rest of the respondents initiated their own early retirement for several other reasons, the most common being monetary. Either they had accumulated enough assets, were attracted by the pension, or had calculated that after taxes the financial incentive to continue working was no longer sufficiently high when compared to the pension. Sixty-five percent of the retirees in the sample indicated that financial reasons influenced their decision to retire. By eliminating the number of persons who had reached mandatory retirement age, this percentage increases to 88 percent.

Respondents often checked more than one reason for deciding to retire early (see Table 3–1). For example, health factors and the stresses and physical demands of their jobs were cited by 58 percent of the respondents. Even so, about one fourth of these people subsequently began working again; a relatively high proportion went into consulting work or became self-employed where, perhaps, the stresses and strains of work were reduced from their preretirement level.

In addition to monetary and health reasons, respondents mentioned other negative feelings about continuing to work in general, or specifically, about their jobs. Thirty-one percent of early retirees said they no longer liked their work, and the same percentage said they felt they had worked long enough.

Among the possible reasons for an individual's initiating a request for retirement is, of course, an offer of employment by another company. It is interesting to note, however, that practically none of those respondents who initiated a retirement request did so because another company had offered them employment. In some cases, it is true, individuals had made arrangements for postretirement salaried employment before they retired, but these plans seem to have been made much more on their own initiative.

Table 3–1   Reasons Given for Early Retirement

Reason	Percentage
Finances	65
Health/job tension	58
Had risen as far as they could	33
No longer liked the job	31
Felt they had worked long enough	31
Layoff/change in management	30
Reached mandatory age	25

Note: Respondents could choose more than one reason.

Retirement Counseling

Retirement counseling offered by the retiree's company is one potential vehicle for reducing strains, both financial and otherwise, that result from poor retirement planning. However, for our sample, this resource does not appear to have fulfilled its potential, as 60 percent of the respondents did not use company-provided counseling to do their planning. About half of those were unaware that the counseling services were even available. Of the others who knew that their company provided counseling, 25 percent did not think it would be useful, and another 19 percent indicated that they did not wish to discuss their personal situation with retirement counselors provided by the company.

After Retirement: Work?

One half of the respondents were interested enough in employment after retirement either to take active steps to secure work or to think about it in a planning sense. Those retirees who had taken steps to secure employment were more likely to be employed and working for pay than those who did not. Some retirees who had not planned on working after retirement found they were forced to work for various reasons. About *two fifths* of the respondents had some kind of work experience during their retirement years, even though the majority admitted they could get along quite well without work.

Type of Work Sought

Many retirees sought consulting jobs or self-employed positions, which they viewed as an escape from the rigid work schedules, conformity to organizational imperatives, and unwelcome stress and conflict associated with their former employment. Some retirees viewed new work not as an escape but as an adventure, as did this respondent: "I believe everyone owes himself a second career. They should retire early (60–65) and launch a new career utilizing their talents in a somewhat different direction or profession in order to enjoy life at its fullest."

The following list illustrates the wide variety of work activity that opened up to the respondents after retirement:

1. Male nurse (says he's in much demand)
2. Stockbroker
3. Manager of a miniature golf course (having a wonderful time)
4. Economist
5. Rancher
6. Teacher ("my raison d'être")
7. Fisherman
8. Psychologist
9. Artist
10. Dance teacher (having a wonderful time)
11. Priest
12. Hotel manager (always wanted to be one)

Two thirds of the respondents were managers before retirement, while three quarters of the respondents who were employed at the time of the survey were engaged in professional or technical work. Of those retirees currently in salaried positions, only one in ten said their postretirement job was similar to their preretirement position. A change in work environment and work role was for some a welcome part of their postretirement work experience. In the words of one respondent, "My biggest problem after retirement was being available around the house for trivial chores I didn't want to do. The work I am doing now provides an escape from this."

Reasons for Seeking Postretirement Work

Many retirees responded that their work before retirement had ceased to provide sufficient challenge and that postretirement work had been a revitalizing experience because it offered new challenges and rich rewards (either financially, physically, or both). For some of the respondents who had accepted relatively undemanding salaried employment after retirement, the very fact that their work was unpressured and their schedule relatively flexible and relaxed was one of the major satisfactions of their postretirement work experience. The following list provides a profile of the postretirement work experience of the respondents:

1. For retirees who had worked forty to fifty hours per week before retirement, modal hours of work were around twenty after retirement.
2. Two out of five retirees worked. Those respondents with more education and higher incomes were more likely to work after retirement.
3. Most retirees who worked got their jobs prior to or shortly after retiring, mostly with smaller firms.
4. Retirees worked because they liked to or for the additional income.
5. Most retirees found their present work to be more satisfying than their preretirement work.
6. Most retirees who were not working did not want to work.

Income also plays a large role in the postretirement work experience. One respondent went from working fifty hours a week before retirement to sixty hours a week at his own business after retirement. But he has no regrets, his work is not only more satisfying but also much more rewarding economically.

Attitudes concerning what constitutes a sufficient postretirement income varied, in that they did not seem to be related to present total family income or to the standard of living the retiree was used to before retirement. No relationship existed between expected postretirement income and the person's annual salary in the year before retirement. The following list summarizes the relationship between preretirement and postretirement incomes of the respondents:

1. Mean preretirement annual earned income in 1978 dollars amounted to $28,800 and total family income to $34,500. The $5,700 difference represented an admixture of spouses' earnings and investment income. Mean family income in the twelve months preceding the survey totaled $19,500.

2. In seven out of ten cases, respondents' preretirement earnings accounted for all of the family's earned income; in the
postretirement period only two out of five respondents
accounted for all of the family's earned income.
3. In eight out of ten cases, income from investments accounted
for 25 percent or less of preretirement total family income.
Postretirement investment income accounted for more than
50 percent of total family income in about the same proportion of families.
4. In one out of three families, pensions and Social Security
benefits accounted for 75 percent or more of total postretirement income.

After Retirement: Leisure?

While many people seek a new work experience upon retirement,
others seek more leisurely activities. Several of the respondents in
our survey devoted their newly acquired free time to volunteer
work, home maintenance, and hobbies.

Volunteer Work

Slightly over half of all respondents participated in voluntary activities before and after retirement, the majority with religious organizations. During the preretirement period, about nine out of ten of
these respondents devoted from one to five hours a week to voluntary activities. As one might expect, their involvement in volunteer
work increased in the postretirement period. One respondent put it
this way: "As for me, I wonder how I would ever find time to go to
work [paid], as I'm so busy working for nursing home committees,
health organization board of directors, trustee for a hospital,
treasurer of church, state church board of directors, and so forth."

Home and Hobbies

In their preretirement years, three out of four respondents spent
under five hours a week on home maintenance; after retirement
over one out of four retirees spent ten or more hours a week on

home maintenance. A comparable shift occurred with respect to domestic chores.

An even more radical shift occurred with respect to time devoted to hobbies. After retirement three out of five respondents reported spending ten hours or more a week on such activities. One respondent wrote:

> *I worked for forty years and enjoyed my work. I retired because there were so many things I had never been able to do because there was no time. Now I can play bridge, raise flowers (I always did), cook and entertain; take a trip when it's not a weekend; belong to church altar guild and daytime church groups; take regular college courses instead of at night—I'm not interested in a degree, but there is a college in my neighborhood and I enroll for subjects that interest me.*

Table 3–2 shows the change in frequency of participation in recreational activities from preretirement to postretirement. With the exception of technical and business-related reading, all of the activities show a significant increase in participation, especially sports, household repair, gardening, and travel. Sports participants were likely to be younger and more satisfied with retirement. They were also more likely to claim that both their health and social life had improved since retirement.

Table 3-2   Change in Frequency of Participation in Recreational Activities

Activity	Percentage
General household repair	+32
Travel	+24
Active sports	+23
Gardening	+19
TV	+14
Reading newspapers	+12
Reading current fiction	+10
Woodworking	+9
Reading nonfiction, card games, arts and crafts	+7
Music, theatre	+4
Photography	+3
Sports events	+2
Painting, adult education	+1
Technical/business reading	−20

Note: The figures represent the percentage of respondents who said they engaged in an activity frequently in the past twelve months of retirement, minus the percentage who engaged in the same activity frequently before retirement.

The Effect of Inflation and Adverse Health on Retirement

Most respondents were not overly surprised by their retirement experiences, with 84 percent saying their experiences were at least fairly similar to what they expected. Surprises tended to be in the areas of inflation and adverse health.

The severity of current inflation, however, was one factor that many respondents had not planned on. Interestingly, those who had underestimated the inflation rate were also those not planning on postretirement work, feeling their financial position was secure. Over a third of the respondents admitted that at the time of retirement they had not given much thought to the average rate of inflation during the rest of their lifetime. Of those respondents who had thought about inflation, 48 percent had severely underestimated its rate—most had predicted the average rate would be under 5 percent. When revenues were unexpectedly affected adversely, the retiree was more likely to return to work. One respondent spoke for many retirees when he described his own circumstances:

> The savings and security plan had delivered to me a very substantial and comforting financial buffer. I used part of it to liquidate all open accounts, to purchase a new car, and to pay off the small unpaid balance of my home mortgage. My wife and I continued to live comfortably by drawing from our "buffer" to augment my pension payments.
>
> The best laid plans of mice and men oft go astray. During the past two or three years, that old devil "inflation" and unheard of increases in local property taxes have drained the balance of our once substantial buffer. We cannot afford to live in our home any longer—in the home that we worked so hard and so long for. We must sell it this year and move, using the sale price to establish another financial buffer, which, hopefully, will carry us through the balance of our lives.

Adverse health also dampened the retirement experience. Only 48 percent of those respondents who had experienced increasingly poor health since retirement said they were satisfied, compared with a satisfied response from 75 percent of those whose postretirement health had improved. Still, in keeping with an overall expectation of worsening health accompanying increasing age, half of the respondents still found retirement satisfactory in spite of poorer health.

Policy Implications of Early Retirement

Policy issues dealing with retired employees, the companies from which they have retired, and governmental policy actions all share a common problem—an overriding concern about the effects of high levels of inflation on our existing patterns of retirement and the economic and social institutions that have grown up around the retirement process. Our respondents clearly state that this issue dominates their retirement experience. Although many retirees have continued to work in their retirement years because they want to work, others have begun to work because of inflation. Many respondents also indicated that they may have to work in the future. Although most of the respondents still feel they retired at about the right time, some admit that inflation is the main reason they are now beginning to feel that they retired too soon.

We have seen that an important concern of many retirees is whether to work. The quality and quantity of that postretirement work is very much an issue. Our respondents generally prefer short, flexible working schedules. Although they are often willing to change their occupation drastically, they resent being forced to do demeaning and low-paid work. In fact, more recent retirees favor professional and technical activities, especially those respondents whose educational attainments were relatively high and whose pre-retirement and postretirement incomes were relatively large.

Corporate Policy Issues

The policy issues relating to early retirement that face the firm subsume most of those facing the individual but are often inverted. The firm necessarily directs most of its energies in human resources to the intake of new members into its labor force—their training, retention, and promotion. Traditionally, the firm has spent much less time on the effective utilization of employees during the years immediately preceding their retirement. Human capital theory may seem to give the firm a powerful argument for the relative neglect of the older members of its labor force. Furthermore, the costs of fringe benefits, particularly defined benefit pension systems, fuel another argument against retaining or hiring older workers.

Age Distribution. The age distribution of a firm's labor force, however, and particularly the age distribution of its managerial and professional/technical staffs, is not something that a firm can arbitrarily set. This age distribution is not only the product of the historical evolution of the firm but also the product of the labor market within which the firm operates. Probably most important, age distribution reflects the technological and organizational imperatives that circumscribe the firm's freedom of action.

Even so, the large corporation may believe that either its existing or its predicted age distribution is an actual or potential problem. How to reconcile the firm's perception of the desired age distributions of its managerial and professional/technical staffs with their actual distribution is bound to raise some difficult policy issues, the most important one being should the firm even have a policy with respect to the age distribution of these staffs? Another one is can the normal course of events and the operation of the labor market be relied on to solve what seems to be potential problems? Here the firm's sense of the potentialities of its labor force, its surrounding labor market, and the capacities of its existing staff to meet whatever stresses and strains may be imposed by the bunching of age distributions by occupation is of critical importance.

Since the firm, even if it might wish to, cannot just dismiss its middle-aged and older managerial personnel—and will be less able to do so in the future—another issue facing the firm is how to make best use of a group of managers and professional/technical personnel, some of whom are facing physical and mental problems associated with increasing age. While it is one thing to cite instances of extraordinary energy, innovativeness, and managerial capacity that can be mustered at very advanced ages, it is another thing to say that all members of older age groups suffer no disabilities. This simply flies in the face of common observation. As they grow older, some people do have less physical and intellectual energy, less flexibility, and less combativeness and competitiveness. But even with these kinds of age deficits, such individuals, because of their experience and their accumulated wisdom, may still be able to make invaluable contributions if an institution knows how to utilize them properly.

Pension Systems.   A particularly thorny set of policy issues is related to the incentive and disincentive effects of pension systems. Employees generally favor a defined benefit pension system because it allows them to know what sums they can expect during their retirement years. They particularly favor a plan whose benefit formula heavily weights the salaries of their last few years of employment. Some plans may also be designed so that early retirement does not lead to actuarially neutral reductions in benefits, a feature that favors employees contemplating early retirement and that provides an incentive to elect early retirement.

The conflict between older workers who want to continue to work and those who want to elect early retirement arises because the defined benefit pension plan provides an incentive—often quite strong—for the firm to substitute younger workers for older workers. The more the pension benefit formula weights salaries in the last years of employment, the greater this incentive is.

What Corporations Can Do.   Corporations, for their part, are concerned about the number of managerial and professional/technical personnel who may elect *not to retire early* in the near future. They are also interested in making use of the skills and experience of some of those employees who have in the past elected early retirement. It is our view that if large corporations would be more flexible in their use of retired personnel (their own and those of other corporations), the pool of early retirees willing to accept a new relationship to their former employers or new employers would maintain itself or possibly grow. Of course, the corporation would have to show initiative and use its preretirement contacts and the stage of the retirement decision itself to let those individuals who are contemplating early retirement know of the corporation's interest in their future work ambitions.

In the face of continuing inflation, which is likely to yield only very slowly (if at all), what can companies do to mitigate the high—and probably still higher—discontent that will arise from the erosion of pension benefits. Some of the stronger companies may be able to provide a cost of living adjustment for some minimum amount of a variable pension. Opportunity should be offered to employees to make voluntary contributions during their years of employment, especially when the needs for current income diminish. By building up a greater equity in their pension, employees will have a partial hedge against erosion from inflation. The last decade has demonstrated that more and more Americans are owners of homes and that such ownership has proved to be a major bulwark against the loss of asset value from inflation. In future corporate approaches to fringe benefit arrangements, the importance of home ownership as an appreciating asset to retirees should be taken into consideration.

Public Policy Issues

Private pension systems with defined benefits are not age neutral in their effects on the supply of and the demand for labor and usually create incentives on the part of the employee to retire and on the part of the employer to dismiss or not hire older workers. Similarly, Social Security policy also has important disincentive effects on older workers in the preretirement stage. The provision of Social Security benefits being drawn at age 62 has had an immediate and pronounced effect on the labor force participation rates of employees reaching that age. Even if the reduction in benefits associated with electing age 62 rather than age 65 were actuarially neutral (which is not the case), the mere fact of being eligible for benefits at age 62 has probably had a strong disincentive effect upon further work.

In other words, if early retirement were the desired goal of public and private policy, the system we now have would be efficacious, even if it were age-neutral. Those individuals on the margin of electing early retirement would be encouraged to do so, and those older employees desiring to keep their jobs would find it harder to do so and would encounter more severe difficulties when they sought reemployment than if they had been dismissed. But early retirement is not necessarily a desired goal. If a productive person retires to continue working in a new field, then it can be beneficial overall; but encouraging complete retirement at an early age reduces the overall size of the labor pool which then, in turn, decreases the potential for further output growth.

Over the recent past, and probably for some time in the future, increases in the amount of Social Security benefits and changes in the benefit formulas will occur. Without reducing any present benefits, Congress could allocate the increase in future benefit levels in ways that will over time substantially alter the incentive effects of the Social Security system. Raising, or eliminating entirely, the ceiling on earned income before reduction in benefits takes place is one obvious step in this direction. Lowering the formula for benefit reduction when the earned income ceiling is reached is another step. Both policies were strongly advocated by many of our respondents. Another change that would decrease, or remove entirely, the disincentive effects of Social Security would be an increase in the size of benefits for every additional year that an employee worked after age 65. Sufficiently large increases would make it possible to achieve some of the objectives that people who advocated increasing the formal retirement age for full benefits from age 65 to 68 have in mind. Changing the incentive structures of private and public pension systems will not be costless. However, what should be kept firmly in the minds of policymakers is the alternative of doing nothing. The trend toward early retirement has been one of the more massive social developments of the last few decades—a trend that has already cost the nation significant amounts of money in the form of the benefits paid to those early retirees and a significant decrease in the national output that their nonparticipation in the labor force has occasioned.

Chapter 4

POSTPONING RETIREMENT

by Harold L. Sheppard

The retirement age debate in the United States has intensified for a number of reasons. Many Americans believe they should have the right to remain in the labor force without regard to chronological age, or at least that 65 is "too young" an age for any compulsory retirement policy; on the other hand, others feel that older workers should retire to make room for younger workers.

Occasionally, the notion of a later retirement age has been introduced as one means of mitigating the potential cost increases arising from early retirement. While raising the age at which an individual is eligible for "full" benefits under Social Security (now 65) may be a "logical" approach, it is one fraught with political booby traps. Certainly a continuation of the current high inflation rate can be expected to cause many employees to reconsider any previous plans or desires they might have had for early retirement.

But what about offering a "bonus" to workers who delay retirement after, say age 65, at a rate still below that which would be counterproductive as far as the solvency of the Social Security system is concerned? While a policy that very gradually raises the age for "full" benefits might possibly be introduced in years to come, a retirement-postponement bonus would entail fewer political pitfalls. Furthermore, a bonus method would be more in keeping with American traditions of not forcing, but motivating, individuals and organizations toward socially desired ends.

The Nature of the Study

This chapter identifies those workers who would be most likely to respond to such an incentive, with a special emphasis on research findings and their implications over the next ten to twenty years. Nearly a thousand men and women in the labor force, age 40 to 69 years old, were interviewed in San Diego and Denver in 1978. The original study was sponsored by the Administration on Aging under a grant to the Center on Work and Aging of the American Institute for Research.[1]

The data base for this chapter is a subsample of approximately 660 persons, which consists of only those workers who were employed without interruption over a period of roughly three years. We are dealing with what might be considered the "mainstream" of American workers. We recognize the possibility that the San Diego and Denver subsample for this report may not be exactly representative of the total U.S. labor force, but we have no reason to believe that these workers are unique or atypical with respect to the national labor force.

The proportion of men in our sample that indicated they would postpone retirement after age 65 in exchange for a "bonus" was 42 percent, which was slightly higher than the proportion of women (38 percent) who responded the same way. Respondents were first asked if Social Security's scheduled 3 percent raise in benefits for each year that full benefits at age 65 are postponed would be enough for them to think about postponing retirement. Second, if they said "no" to that question, they were then asked how much of a bonus would be necessary for them to consider postponing retirement. Respondents who said "yes" to the first question and provided some figure in answering the second are defined here as meeting our first requirement for candidacy for retirement postponement.

Primarily as a means of isolating the more serious respondents within the group interested in such a postponement bonus, we added a requirement that they approve of the legislative proposal to raise the allowable mandatory retirement age from 65 to 70. Their opinions were sought in March 1978, before actual passage of those amendments. Compared to the responses to the first question, substantially higher proportions of both men and women approved of this proposal (65 and 72 percent, respectively). Considering the fact that no more than one fifth of the sample were employed in establishments with a fixed retirement-age policy, these high percentages of employees approving of the increase in age suggest that the principle involved has a wide appeal that goes beyond the individual's own employment situation.

Our focus in this study is on a typology based on the combined responses to the two questions, especially those men and women who would (1) postpone retirement with an appropriate incentive and (2) approve of the general principle of raising the legally permitted age of mandatory retirement. (See Table 4–1 for the relationship between the two criteria.) Twenty-nine percent of both men and women would postpone retirement and approve of raising the mandatory retirement age.[2]

Economic and Demographic Characteristics

Our purpose here is to present the rates of "candidacy" for retirement postponement by selected economic, demographic, attitudinal, and other characteristics. For reasons that will become clear as this presentation proceeds, men and women are reported separately.

Industry

Both male and female workers in such service industries as personal services and entertainment had the highest proportions (above average) of candidates for postponed retirement (see Table 4–2). In finance, insurance, and real estate only women had an above-average candidate proportion (39 percent).

Only 15 percent of the men in construction would apparently opt for postponed retirement, in contrast with 29 percent of all the men in our sample. Contrary to our own expectations, the proportion of men in manufacturing who were candidates was identical to that for the total male sample (about 29 percent), while the female rate for manufacturing was the lowest for the entire sample (12.5 percent).

Table 4–1 Relationship Between Acceptance of Retirement-Postponement Bonus and Approval of Increasing Mandatory Retirement Age

	Approve of Age Increase		Disapprove of Age Increase	
	Men	*Women*	*Men*	*Women*
Would accept bonus	48.3%	41.2%	30.8%	29.5%
Number of cases	230	204	120	78

Table 4-2   Candidacy Rates by Industry (in Percent)

Industry	Men	Women
Construction	15.0	—
Manufacturing	28.9	12.5
Public utilities and transportation	27.3	16.7
Wholesale and retail trade	26.8	30.6
Finance, insurance, and real estate	29.6	39.1
Business and personal services, and entertainment	50.0	39.1
Professional	36.5	33.3
Public administration	30.7	14.3
Total	28.7	28.7

Occupation

The unexpected finding about men in manufacturing is probably more a function of occupation than of industry. Manufacturing is not synonymous with "blue collar," and when we examine directly the blue-collar males and females, we find that the proportion likely to postpone retirement is the lowest for all occupations (see Table 4–3). Only 22 percent of the male blue-collar workers were candidates, in contrast to 39 percent of the "lower-white-collar" men (in sales and clerical jobs). The corresponding percentages among women were 19 percent for blue-collar workers and 32 percent for lower-white-collar workers.

Income

Assuming that annual family income of workers has some influence on future income as retirees, we should expect to find that lower-income persons will tend to be most attracted to incentives to re-

Table 4-3   Candidacy Rates by Occupation (in Percent)

Occupations	Men	Women
Professional and technical	31.9	29.4
Managers	28.4	36.0
"Other" white-collar	39.4	31.6
Blue-collar	22.0	18.5
Services, nonprivate, household	25.0	21.1
Total	29.5	28.7

main in the labor force. That is, of course, what we found in our sample, regardless of sex (see Table 4–4).

The importance of income is much more pronounced (especially in the case of males) when the focus is merely on the financial bonus for postponing retirement, without consideration of the retirement age issue. More than 50 percent of the men with less than $20,000 annual family income, compared with only 37 percent of those with at least $20,000 annual family income, were interested in a bonus. Even among women the data suggest that the critical determinant in postponing retirement is the bonus factor rather than approval or disapproval of the extension of the allowable mandatory retirement age. In fact, attitudes about this issue seem to be unrelated to income.

Age

Age appears to provide no explanation for any differences in candidacy, especially among women (see Table 4–5). If there is any relationship between age and postponement among men, it is in an unexpected direction: the younger the worker, the greater the odds for being a later retirement candidate. Such differences, however, were not proven to be statistically significant.

Given the current controversy over the possible effects that the recent amendments to the Age Discrimination in Employment Act may have on the job chances of younger workers, some additional findings are reported here. Any definitive conclusions, however,

Table 4–4 Candidacy Rates by Family Income Level (in Percent)

Income	Men	Women
Under $20,000	33.1	32.2
$20,000-plus	25.5	25.4

Table 4–5 Candidacy Rates by Workers' Age (in Percent)

Age	Men	Women
40–44	35.4	24.6
45–49	30.8	29.9
50–54	25.9	28.8
55–69	25.7	30.7

must be tempered by the fact that our sample consists of persons no younger than 40 years old.

Nevertheless, it might be argued that workers as young as 40 to 44 years, for example, could feel that their promotional chances would be limited by any extension of the allowable mandatory retirement age. If this is the case, we should expect to find that younger workers in our sample have the lowest approval of the shift from 65 to 70 in mandatory retirement age. Contrary to such expectations, however, the youngest group of men in our sample— those 40 to 44 years old—had the *highest* rate of approval (75 percent) compared with 63 percent of all other men in the sample. This difference in proportions was statistically significant at the .05 level (see Table 4–6).

The picture is somewhat opposite among women: The *oldest* group (those 55 years and older) had the greatest rate of approval. Nevertheless, the youngest group of women (those 40 to 44 years) did not have the lowest approval rate, contrary to what might have been expected. In other words, our findings do not provide support for the notion that compared to older workers, younger workers oppose the 1978 legislation because of any self-interest in the jobs that older workers occupy.

Even more directly related to this issue are the surprising responses to the statement "Older workers should retire when they can, so as to give younger people more of a chance on the job." Any relationship of the worker's age to his or her position on this question was opposite to what might be expected: The older workers approved in proportions greater than the younger ones (see Table 4–7).

On a speculative level, these unexpected findings may be due to the possibility that younger workers (at least those in their early 40s) are more altruistic than otherwise believed. These workers could also be concerned about how they will benefit from an extension of mandatory retirement age when they themselves become "older" workers. They may thus look for labor market or personnel practices that do not force them to retire simply to create vacancies for younger workers.

It should not be surprising to find that candidates for deferred retirement (males and females alike) had the highest percentage rejecting the suggestion that older workers should retire to make room for younger ones.

Table 4–6   Workers in Agreement with Increase in Mandatory Retirement Age (in Percent)

Age	Men	Women
40–44	74.7	71.0
45–49	58.6	75.8
50–54	67.1	61.1
55–69	63.8	81.4

Table 4–7   Workers in Agreement that Older Workers Should Retire to Give Younger People a Chance (in Percent)

Age	Men	Women
40–44	35.0	42.9
45–49	46.2	37.8
50–54	46.2	47.2
55+	49.5	50.0

Other research found that among the steadily employed, agreement with the policy of retirement by older workers to make room for younger ones was considerably higher among workers in the high unemployment area (San Diego) than in the low unemployment area (Denver).[3]

With respect to these findings, an interesting commentary on the American scene is that during our most recent recession periods, few, if any, voices were heard that advocated legislative action to provide earlier retirement under Social Security as a means of "solving" the unemployment problem. Such an advocacy was, and still is, prominent in several European countries yet, ironically, the overt impetus for raising the allowable compulsory retirement age to 70 emerged in Congress during the 1973–1975 recession.

Marital Status

Because nearly all of the men in our sample were married (94 percent), it is difficult to draw any conclusions about the role of marital status on the retirement-postponement tendencies among men (see Table 4–8). There is a suggestion, however, that unmarried men are more likely to have such tendencies than married men. Slightly less than 29 percent of the married men were de-

Table 4-8   Candidacy Rates by Marital Status (in Percent)

Marital Status	Men	Women
Married	28.8	25.0
Not married	36.0	36.1
Separated and divorced	—	29.1
Widowed	—	45.2
Never married	—	45.5

layed-retirement candidates, compared with 36 percent of the un-married men.

The case is more clear-cut among women, however. Only two thirds of the women were married, with husband present in the household. Only 25 percent of the married women were candidates, compared with 36 percent of those who were not married—that is, separated, divorced, widowed, or never married. This difference is statistically significant at the .05 level.

To the extent that women increasingly become members of the labor force and that they may remain unmarried throughout their lives or become divorced or widowed, it may be reasonable to project a future in which current retirement age policies may be less accepted than they previously were. The same scenario might also be expected to apply to men. The reasons for our findings and our portrait of the future are both economic and psychological in nature. Married couples in which both partners are in the labor force tend to have a higher level of financial retirement resources, while un-married individuals may tend to derive greater psychological re-wards from work continuity as well as social contacts at work.

Education

Our findings on the relationship between years of schooling and candidacy for postponing retirement simply confirm national and smaller sample data: Higher participation rates and lower retire-ment rates exist among higher-educated men and women (see Table 4–9).

What is remarkable about our own findings is the lack of male-female difference in candidacy rates by level of schooling. Among men and women with at least one year of college, almost one third are candidates for postponing retirement.

Table 4–9 Candidacy Rates by Education (in Percent)

Level of Schooling	Men	Women
Under twelve years	19.7	15.4
High school degree	29.6	29.8
One or more years of college	32.1	31.3

Better health in later years, the prospects of continued high inflation rates, and the improved educational levels of workers in future years may outweigh other factors that have, in recent years, served to accelerate rates of retirement.

Dependents

In much of our research we have been interested in the issue of how much influence the number of dependents has on the retirement intentions and expectations of workers, especially of family heads. Among the workers in our sample without dependents, only 22 percent were candidates for early retirement, compared with 33 percent of workers with one or more dependents. The relationship between absence or presence of dependents to candidacy for later retirement is especially marked among the men in the sample (19 percent without dependents, compared with 34 percent with dependents). In the case of women, the "cut-off point" is clearly among those with three or more dependents. Among these women, nearly 46 percent are later-retirement candidates, compared to only 26 percent of those with two or fewer dependents.

This analysis, of course, does not take into consideration the age of the worker, but we still are of the opinion that the total number of children ever born and reared by workers affects what we call their "retirement resources." The greater the number of dependents, the lower such resources. Furthermore, even though persons in the future reaching the *current* retirement ages can be expected to have fewer children than their counterparts in recent years had, we might also expect that they will postpone childbearing to an age later than the current pattern. If that is the case, we can expect a higher proportion of older workers with children still at home, in college, or only recently beyond dependent status. These factors all affect the financial capacity of such older workers.

In addition, financial responsibilities for children are not necessarily reduced arithmetically with respect to the size of a family.
According to Paul Demeny of the Population Council, "Parents
might have smaller families and yet spend just as much in total on
children, or even more than when larger families were the norm."[4]

Pension Coverage

We had expected to find that workers without any private pension
coverage (over and above Social Security) would be more likely to
be candidates for retirement postponement. But our data did not
definitely confirm that expectation. Among the men in the sample,
coverage versus no coverage made no difference at all. There was a
slightly higher proportion of women without such coverage who
were candidates (33 percent), but this proportion was not clearly
statistically different from that among women who were covered by
a pension (25 percent).

We should report, however, that when the focus of analysis is on
the "bonus" variable alone, a difference in percentages in the case of
women does appear. Only 33 percent of the women covered by a
pension reported that such a bonus would be an incentive to postpone retirement after age 65, compared to 43 percent among those
without any pension coverage.

Social-Psychological Factors

The previous section concentrated on such "objective" economic
and demographic variables as industry, occupation, income, education, and so forth. But human behavior, decision making, and intentions can also be influenced by sociopsychological variables.

Acceptance of Universal Fixed Retirement Age

How an individual feels about the notion of a fixed retirement age
for everyone will depend on his or her own propensity to extend
retirement age. We should first report that over 80 percent of both
men and women disagreed with any universal fixed retirement age.
In fact, about 45 percent disagreed *strongly*—that high a per-

centage of strong disagreement is unusual in opinion surveys in general.

As might be expected, the few persons who agreed with a fixed retirement age policy can hardly be classified as candidates for postponed retirement (see Table 4–10). Our preliminary data suggest that workers against both notions used as our candidacy criteria are also substantially in favor of a universal fixed age for retirement.

Preferred Retirement Age

Here again, we should expect to find that candidacy rate and the age at which the worker prefers to retire are related to each other. The statistical analysis unquestionably confirms this expectation, especially among the men (see Table 4–11). The older the preferred retirement age, the greater the rate of candidacy for postponing retirement.

Table 4–10 Candidacy Rates by Agreement-Disagreement with Universal Fixed Retirement Age (in Percent)

Response	Men	Women
Agree	10.0	18.8
	(70)	(307)
Disagree	34.0	31.0
	(48)	(239)

Note: Number of cases in parentheses.

Table 4–11 Candidacy Rates by Preferred Retirement Age (in Percent)

Preferred Retirement Age	Men	Women
Before 65	25.1	17.8
	(195)	(152)
65	36.1	44.7
	(52)	(38)
After 65	46.9	50.0
	(32)	(22)
Non-Age Answers	33.3	34.9
	(75)	(63)

Note: Number of cases in parentheses.

Summary and Conclusions

This study explored the attributes that are associated with the willingness of middle-aged and older workers to consider a financial incentive for postponing retirement (over and above the income gained through additional years of earnings) in the form of increased Social Security benefits. In examining the attributes that appear to be associated with that willingness (and as a crude but useful form of projections concerning the future of retirement age policy in our country) consideration should be given to whether a given attribute (when appropriate) will characterize American society and its work force more in the future than is presently the case.

Changing retirement age policies and practices will, in our opinion, undoubtedly characterize the next ten to twenty years in American personnel and industrial relations. The previous trend toward early (pre-65) retirement will, at the very least, stabilize and be accompanied by an opposite pattern—namely, an increasing number of workers opting to remain in the labor force longer than their older relatives and counterparts. This new pattern will emerge partly out of economic necessity and partly out of the changing characteristics (demographic and psychological) that enter into retirement behavior, regardless of historical time period.

At the same time, we might expect a growing attention in Congress and elsewhere to proposals for some form of a gradual increase in the age for retirement under Social Security (at least for "full" benefits) as one means of alleviating the rising expenditures for benefits of retired workers (and their dependents). To the extent that the population of such workers increases more than expected (a result of the increasing life expectancy of persons age 60 to 65), those expenditures might come under closer scrutiny.

We have some preliminary data that bear on the critical issue of the degree of receptivity on the part of workers to such proposals. Workers in our sample who agreed that the Social Security system was "in trouble" (approximately 80 percent of the overall sample) were also asked whether they approved or disapproved of some suggested solutions, one of which included "gradually raising retirement age to keep the number of retired persons from growing so fast." The findings indicate that the following three types of workers tend to approve of such a proposal the most: (1) all but blue-collar workers, (2) college educated workers, and (3) candidates for retirement postponement.

Perhaps as the population comes to consist less and less of blue-collar workers and acquires higher educational levels, proposals of such a nature may be considered more seriously by the electorate.

At any rate, on the level of the individual, inflation appears to be producing changes in one's expected retirement age—perhaps for the first time in several decades, in an upward direction. If and when individual motives coincide with governmental and other institutional recognition of the aggregate macro-benefits of an increase in the national average retirement age, we might witness a somewhat dramatic shift in the country's retirement age policy.

Endnotes

1. Harold L. Sheppard and Sara E. Rix, *The Employment Environment and Older Worker Job Experiences,* Final Report (Washington, D.C.: American Institute for Research, April 1979).
2. While not treated separately in this report, we should note that approximately one fifth of the total sample of men and women were (1) not interested in any incentive for postponing retirement and (2) against increasing the allowable mandatory retirement age.
3. Sheppard and Rix, *Employment Environment.*
4. Paul Demeny, cited in "The Burgeoning Benefits of a Lower Birth Rate," *Business Week,* December 15, 1973.
5. The question was worded: "Many people feel that there should be a fixed retirement age for everyone. How strongly do you agree or disagree with that statement?"
6. See H. L. Sheppard and S. E. Rix, *The Graying of Working America: The Coming Crisis of Retirement-Age Policy* (New York: Free Press–Macmillan, 1977, 1979), for an extended discussion of the economic, biomedical, and demographic factors that may lead to a reanalysis of current retirement-age policy.

Chapter 5

THE ECONOMIC AND SOCIAL EFFECTS OF HOURS REDUCTION

by John D. Owen

Contrary to popular opinion, the "average workweek" really has not decreased in the past forty years. Rather, a modest decline has occurred in *measured* hours. The average weekly hours of nonagricultural employees went from 40.9 in 1948 to 38.5 in 1977. This drop, however, appears to reflect changes in the composition of the labor force rather than a reduction in the hours worked by individuals or groups that compose the work force.

Trends in Hours Worked

A larger proportion of the work force is composed of women and students: Female nonagricultural employees made up less than 29 percent of the work force in 1940 and constitute over 41 percent of it today; students made up 1 percent or less of the work force in 1940 but now comprise over 6 percent. Because of group differences in the number of hours worked[1]—women average 34 hours per week, male students 23 hours, and nonstudent males about 43 hours—the declining proportion of nonstudent males in the labor force has produced a *statistical* decline in average weekly hours worked.

Hours data for the largest group, nonstudent males, actually show a slight increase from 1948 to 1969 (two years of relatively full employment) and a slight decline from 1969 to 1977 (a period of persistently high unemployment). Over the whole period, however, there was no net change, as seen from Table 5–1.

Table 5-1   Weekly Hours of Work, Nonstudent Males, 1948–1977

Year	Unadjusted	Adjusted for Growth in Vacations and Holidays
1948	42.7	41.6
1950	42.2	41.0
1953	42.5	41.4
1956	43.0	41.8
1959	42.0	40.7
1962	43.1	41.7
1966	43.5	42.1
1969	43.5	42.0
1972	42.9	41.4
1975	42.4	40.8
1976	42.4	40.9
1977	42.8	41.3

The hours of work series for nonstudent men may be biased because it omits the effects of increases in holidays and vacations. When an adjustment is made for this, no significant change is found in hours worked in the 1948–1969 period. A slight decline is observed in the next few years as unemployment increases. These data are the best available. Each month a random sample of Americans is asked how many vacation days they enjoyed in the preceding week. When aggregated over the year, a rough measure of annual vacations is obtained. A much more generous view is derived from collective bargaining agreements. However, these data are biased upward because (1) union contracts provide above-average vacations; (2) many years of seniority in a particular firm are required before an employee receives maximum vacation time; and (3) many employees work part or all of their paid vacation time.[2] Even if the Bureau of Labor Statistics' data understate vacations by as much as one week, just a 2 percent additional reduction in work time would take place—hardly a significant decline in hours worked.

The abrupt end of the downward trend movement in weekly hours of work after World War II, in combination with the continued upward trend in female labor force participation, have both contributed to a leveling off, or possibly an increase, in the number of hours supplied to the labor market by the average married couple in their prime years. This trend appears to be in sharp contrast to trends toward true reductions in working times that extend back as far as the early 19th century.

Data for the 19th century are not as good as the more recent numbers, but the downward trend in hours worked does appear to go back to the early decades of that century when the numbers of hours worked were very high.

Progress toward fewer hours of work characterized the entire period from 1900 to 1948, although this progress was more rapid in some decades than in others. The 1900–1914 interval saw vigorous pressure to reduce the number of hours worked in many industries. Government control over hours during World War I and the favorable consideration given to union demands during this period led to further reductions. After the war, unions were greatly weakened in some industries that had earlier obtained the eight-hour day; hours were actually increased in many of these industries in the 1920s, though generally not to pre–World War I levels. However, the 1920s saw continued progress toward hours reduction in other industries. The greatest progress was made in the iron and steel and in the canning and preserving industries, which were nonunionized and where the number of working hours had been very high.

The number of hours worked weekly in the 1930s followed a somewhat different pattern. After a virtual collapse of hours schedules from 1929 to 1934 as a result of the Great Depression, hours recovered moderately in the late 1930s and then rose to a rather high level in the overtime economy of World War II. After the war, when they declined to a more normal level in 1948, they simply appeared to be continuing a long-term downward trend.[3] Thus, there seems to be little basis in the earlier history of hours worked for predicting the leveling off that occurred after World War II.

Why Hours of Work Leveled Off

An explanation of the leveling off of hours worked since World War II is essential for a forecast of future changes. Economists generally reject the popular view that the number of hours worked is primarily determined by laws and by trade unions; they instead argue that the number of hours is influenced more by underlying market forces affecting employer and employee preferences, which in turn determine the labor market results. This emphasis on market forces is partly due to the fact that most of the decline in hours of work took place under very competitive labor market conditions in the 19th and early 20th centuries. During that time there were no effective national laws controlling hours and only an insignificant number of ineffective trade unions. In a competitive market it appears reasonable to assume—as a simplifying approximation—that entrepreneurs will try to minimize their labor costs by seeking out the hours schedule that will enable them to hire the best labor at the cheapest unit cost. The discussion of past trends in hours of work in this section follows this assumption.

Changes in the Absolute Return to Effort

In applying the competitive model, economists have treated the growth in real wages as the principal factor involved in changing the number of hours worked. The crux of the argument is that higher wages enable workers to satisfy their more pressing wants for food, clothing, housing, and so forth *and* to fulfill their demands for time off by opting for a somewhat shorter workweek. This shorter workweek will reduce their weekly incomes, though not to the level prevailing before the wage increase. The rational employer will reduce work schedules as the hourly wage is increased, since the competitive theory predicts that those employers who reduce hours first can have a competitive edge over other employers in obtaining labor.

However, the analysis here is complicated: A wage hike raises the income of the worker, which produces a positive "income effect" on the demand for leisure; but this hike also increases the opportunity cost, or *price*, of an hour of leisure, which produces a negative "substitution" effect on the demand for leisure. In theory this "substitution" effect could be just as strong as (or even stronger than) the "income" effect, so that a rise in wages would have no impact on the number of hours worked (or could actually produce an increase in hours).

But in practice, the long period in which work hours declined as wages increased convinced many observers that the income effect dominated. Still, the role of substitution is thought to be important, in that it explains why only a small portion of gains in real hourly wages has been absorbed by leisure. During the rapid decline in hours worked in the late 19th and early 20th centuries, a quarter or less of the potential growth in consumption went to reduced hours, and the remainder went to consumer goods and services.

Changes in the Relative Return to Effort

Declining Returns and Declining Hours.   While the traditional analysis fits the facts well enough when hours worked were declining, it fails to explain the leveling off of hours that has occurred over the past several decades. One reason for this failure is the implicit assumption that the worker's effective labor input (and hence, by the traditional theory, his or her wage income) will increase in strict proportion to the number of hours he or she works. This assumption is not essential to the competitive view of determining the number of hours worked and is generally not valid; even if the employee is paid in accordance with his or her effective labor input, the latter will generally *not* vary in strict proportion to the number of hours worked. As an example, critics of the progressive income tax and of the present welfare system argue that both systems reduce the ratio of the marginal to the average return to effort—that is, the relative return to effort—and hence tend to discourage work.

There are other important examples of declining relative return to effort. At the beginning of the long downward movement in hours of work in the early 19th century, many workers were at true subsistence levels. The *relative* return to a worker from long hours of work was very high indeed. If workers worked less and earned less, they would likely die of malnutrition or of one of the diseases of poverty. As wages increased, it was no longer necessary to work as many hours just to survive.

Increasing Returns and Stable Hours.   The relative return to effort theory also provides a more positive explanation for the recent leveling off of hours worked. Certain factors in our affluent society now act to *increase* the marginal above the average return to effort and hence raise the relative return. Individuals, and society as a whole, now make an enormous fixed investment in the education of the average young American. Only if graduates put in relatively long hours at a job can they economically justify the financial investment their families and society have made in their schooling—an investment that must be spread over a large number of lifetime hours of paid employment. The argument is that better educated employees will work longer hours than their less educated counterparts. Indeed, cross-sectional data usually confirm this. Moreover, the argument predicts that when outlays for education increase rapidly, hours for working tend to stabilize or even increase. In other periods when schooling outlays were growing more slowly, the number of hours worked were more likely to decline.

The figures below show the regression results of an attempt to isolate the relative importance of real hourly compensation *and* real education outlays (per member of the work force) in determining weekly hours worked in the 1900–1975 period.

	Impact on Hours of Percentage Point Rise in Earnings or Education Costs
Hourly earnings	− .20
Education costs	+ .10

As expected, education costs have a positive association with hours of work, and the hourly wage rate has a negative association.[4]

This statistical relationship can now be used to help us understand the stability that has taken place since World War II. The post–World War II years followed one and a half decades of depression and war. Consumption needs of all sorts had gone unmet in those years of unemployment and shortages. In the early days after the war, workers tried to catch up on their purchases of clothing, household appliances, and other consumer goods. There was very little demand for a reduction in work hours.

However, some longer-lasting effects resulted from the catching-up process. For example, birth rates, at a very low level in the 1930s, rose sharply with the return of prosperity in the war and postwar periods. This type of "catching up" had long-term effects on American work and consumption patterns because unlike the purchase of a refrigerator or a car, the decision to have a child imposes costs on a family that extend for two decades.[5]

The effects of the baby boom were further exacerbated by another postwar development—namely, the "education revolution," which increased the average years of schooling by about three and increased the proportion of high school graduates going on to college to a near majority. This vast increase in education investment is believed by some observers to be a reaction to labor market conditions, which generated a higher level of demand for college-trained labor and an increasing level of unemployment for those with below-average schooling. In any event, the extension of schooling greatly increased the average cost of raising a child.

Since the combination of the baby boom and the education revolution increased total education costs considerably in the postwar
period, the enormous outlays required to meet these costs diverted
resources from other consumption and savings and made a reduction in working hours and the ensuing loss of income less attractive.

Figure 5–1 shows actual hours of work for full-employment peak
years and predicted hours of work from the regression. In the post–
World War II period, rapid rises in the real hourly wage rate and
soaring child-rearing costs tended to offset each other. Thus, the
leveling off in hours worked over the past twenty-five years is cor-
rectly predicted. Moreover, when education outlays are ignored, a
decline of *one-half day* in working time is incorrectly forecast for the
post–World War II period.

Training and Experience.   The relative return to effort has also
been influenced by other types of investment in "human capital"
through on-the-job training and experience. One widely respected
estimate puts the value of these postschool investments at about four
fifths of the cost of formal education itself.[6] This investment provides another incentive to increase hours of work, so that the fixed

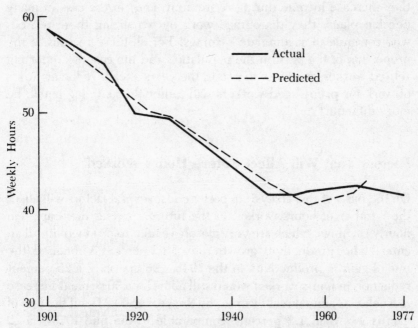

Figure 5-1   Long-Term Movements in Hours of Work for Adult Male, Nonagricultural Employees (Adjusted for Vacations and Holidays)

cost of acquiring these skills can also be spread over a larger number of work hours. One important difference that on-the-job training and experience has compared with formal education, though, is that employers frequently underwrite much of the cost of post-school training. Thus the employers have a special incentive to increase the hours worked, so that they can recoup their share of the investment cost. Some economists believe that the aggregate level of training investment per worker has increased over the past several decades—a trend that would further contribute to the leveling off of hours worked.

The Graying of America. That Americans can now look forward to a longer retirement, based on leaving work earlier and living longer, may also contribute to the stabilization of hours. The relatively low market value of time in a worker's later years, compared with the relatively high value of time in a person's prime years, would be expected to lead to a *rearrangement* of working time, with more working hours per week in the earlier years to provide for the years of low earnings potential. Social Security and private pension schemes both reflect and reinforce this pattern. They reduce take-home income during working years (thereby encouraging work), they increase income during retirement, and, in the case of many pension plans, they discourage work by penalizing those retirees who continue to accumulate earnings. For all these reasons, if the proportion of the aged in the population and the cost of supporting retired workers continue to rise in the years ahead, reducing hours of work for prime-aged workers will (other things being equal) be more difficult.[7]

Factors That Will Affect Future Hours Worked

On the basis of this analysis of past trends, several factors will affect the number of hours worked in the future. Among them are real hourly earnings, which are very closely related to productivity. If an annual labor productivity growth rate of 3.2 percent is obtained (the rate of gain in productivity in the 1948–1969 period), a 25 percent reduction in hours worked would still allow for a 50 percent increase in weekly or annual real incomes by the year 2000.[8] But if the rate of gain is less than 1.3 percent (comparable to the mid-1970s), a 25 percent reduction in hours of work would actually reduce income.[9]

In addition, low birth rates, a leveling off of the increase in number of years spent in school, a reversal of the trend toward early retirement, and continued increases in the labor force participation of women would all help raise the ratio of the working to the non-working population and hence make it easier to reduce the number of hours worked without reducing the living standards.

Another factor leading to shorter hours of work is the continued trend toward a "welfare state," which would impose severe economic costs on society. The extent to which these costs are felt by individuals, however, depends on government policy. Through the welfare system, the government now provides a floor for those individuals who choose not to work, at a fairly generous level by historical standards. In addition, there is a trend toward providing many consumer goods and services free of charge or at highly subsidized prices. Education, medical care, and outdoor recreation are three such examples. At the same time, progressive income taxes may also diminish incentives to work. This welfare state trend could conceal the social costs of a reduction-in-work effort. Individual workers, or even industrywide unions, might opt for fewer hours of work when they realize much of the social cost would be shifted to other workers whose tax rates would be increased as receipts from the taxes of short-schedule workers dropped.

Finally, changes in individual "tastes" may promote a reduction in hours of work. For example, a future change in the emphasis that Americans put on the quantity of leisure or consumption time, relative to the quantity of goods and services used in consumption, could easily produce a downward trend in hours of work.[10]

The factors just presented as possibly affecting the number of hours worked in the future can be summarized in the form of four major scenarios:

1. *No change in hours accompanied by low growth of per capita income.* This scenario would be most probable if productivity grew slowly. Other factors that would contribute to modest income growth include larger than expected increases in longevity, earlier retirements, and a possible end to the rise of female labor force participation. An increase in the birth rate would have the same effect by temporarily raising the dependency ratio—that is, the ratio of the nonworking to the working population.

2. *No change in hours accompanied by high growth in per capita income.* If productivity rose rapidly, while the female labor force participation rate also climbed, and retirement age was stabilized or increased, per capita income would rise rapidly.

3. *A sharp reduction in hours (to thirty or thirty-two hours per week) accompanied by a rapid growth in per capita income.* A reduction in hours would be at least as likely a reaction to continued high productivity. The reduction of hours worked is more likely to take the form of more days off per week than fewer daily hours of work. However, this hours reduction need not mean a discrete jump to the four-day week. Instead, days off per year could be gradually increased (as in the 1976 United Auto Workers contract) until a de facto four-day workweek—say two hundred working days a year—was achieved.

4. *A sharp reduction in hours accompanied by a slow rate of growth in per capita income.* This fourth scenario could have the most negative economic effect. While it may appear to be an unlikely forecast at this time, it could result from a number of factors. For example, a future decline in the "work ethic" or movement toward a welfare state could conceivably yield this scenario. However, past history indicates that a much more likely cause would be a sustained period of high unemployment. It is worthwhile to recall that our basic hours law (the Fair Labor Standards Act of 1938) was passed after several years of very high unemployment but was then retained when the economy returned to normal employment levels.

The Effect of Hours Reduction on Labor Input

Would fewer hours of work lead to more effort per hour and therefore reduce the negative impact, or fatigue effect, on effective labor input? Or how about the effect that a reduction in hours would have on the schooling the work force receives? These and other questions relate to the future implications of hours reduction.

The Fatigue Problem

It seems likely that there would be some—but not very much—diminution of fatigue as hours of work decreased. Much of our rationale for believing in a fatigue effect is based on experience accumulated over a century of hours reduction, as hours declined from very high levels to the present forty to fifty hours per week. Hence, our rationale is limited in its validity when we consider the effects of a reduction in hours to thirty or thirty-two hours a week. Moreover, this historical evidence is not scientifically based. Typically, when hours of work were reduced, other factors changed also. Sometimes machinery or other capital was substituted for labor, or management increased the proportion of effort that it devoted to obtaining better results from labor.

While there is very limited evidence available to suggest that some relief from fatigue is possible (for example, output often declines in the last hours of even an eight-hour day), there are several reasons for believing that this effect is of small magnitude. If hours worked are cut per day, daily setup costs will constitute a powerful offset, especially in industrial jobs. There is also reason to believe that reduction in hours would result eventually in a four-day workweek and *not* a six-hour workday. The four-day week may not relieve fatigue at all, in that there is no persuasive evidence that three-day weekends are beneficial in relieving fatigue.

Evidence from the Part-Time Labor Market

While there is a dearth of information as to what would happen if hours of work were reduced for all workers, considerable data are available on the 20-odd percent of the labor force that now works part time. This part-time labor market provides a major (or possibly extreme) example of the effects that fewer hours of work would likely have on productivity.

The deductions we can draw from this group of workers do not lead to an optimistic conclusion of the effects of a general reduction in hours. Part-timers are generally regarded as less productive than full-timers and are accordingly paid less (or where such hourly wage differentials are contrary to company practice, managers recruit part-timers with superior education, experience, or other qualities at the same hourly wage rate as full-timers). Moreover, part-timers often do not receive the same fringe benefits as do full-timers.

There are economies of scale in hours of work: the fixed costs per employee of hiring, screening, and training must be prorated over the term of employment. Since these costs have to be spread over fewer hours, the net productivity of the part-timer is reduced. A second, complementary reason for the lower productivity of part-timers derives from the fact that more workers must be employed to carry out the same work, thus increasing supervisory, communications, and coordination costs.

The existing data on present part-timers probably understate the negative effects of fewer hours of work. If hours of work for *all* jobs are reduced by 20 or 25 percent, the impact would be much worse. Employers would no longer be able to cream the market—that is, use "overqualified" college students or homemakers for their short-hour jobs. Even more important is the fact that short-timers would not be confined to a few positions where their schedules would cause the least problems (or where they would even be an advantage). Instead, they would be used in mainstream jobs, even in very complex situations, which could drastically reduce labor efficiency.

Education Effects

In addition, a reduction in hours could have negative effects on the schooling that the work force receives and, hence, on its productivity. The crux of the argument is that a reduction in hours would lower the financial rate of return to schooling and, thereby, reduce investment in education. The few available studies indicate that investment in human capital is responsive to changes in its financial rate of return. A widely used, simplified formula for this rate of return is:

$$r = \frac{(w_1 - w_2)H}{C},$$

where w_1 and w_2 are the hourly wages earned with and without an additional year of schooling, respectively; H is the number of hours worked per year after graduation; C is the cost of an additional year of schooling; and r is the financial rate of return to the extra year of schooling. A 25 percent decline in hours of work would yield, other things being equal, a 25 percent decline in the financial rate of return to education.

The Overall Effect

Thus, consideration of the fatigue effect, experience from the part-time labor market, and the possible impact of hours reduction on education all yield a rather negative forecast of the consequences of reduced hours of work. Two possible qualifications should be considered, though, before an assessment is finally made. First, it is often argued that a reduction in hours per worker would increase the number of people who would work. Some women, students, and older workers could handle a thirty-hour workweek, but not a forty-hour workweek. The part-time job market has been growing rapidly; for example, about 40 percent of all new jobs for women in the past twenty years have been part time. Further strengthening and upgrading of this part-time job market would seem to be a more prudent method of attracting marginal workers into the labor force than would a reduction in the standard hours of the majority, mainstream work force, the larger and generally more productive group.

A second and more important offset to hours reduction could be expected to occur if hours of work were to be reduced by law rather than by individuals willing to trade income for leisure. Under these circumstances, many potential secondary earners—namely, women, students, and older workers—would be expected to enter the labor force to compensate for the lower earning of primary members. Workers would also seek out moonlighting opportunities. Similarly, more overtime work would be expected. Hence, in this "evasion" scenario, hours of work supplied to the labor market might not decline as much.

However, ignoring the "evasion" scenario, it would appear most likely that a 20 to 25 percent reduction in hours of work from the present level would yield a decline in effective labor input of at least that magnitude or perhaps even larger.

The Effect of Curtailing Labor Input Through Hours Reduction

The effects of cutting hours on national output depend in part on the interaction with the nation's capital stock. A standard argument in favor of hours reduction is that it will yield a less than proportional decline in output since capital can, to some extent, be substituted for labor. However, this abstract argument has very little application to the concrete case of a reduction in hours.

In the Short Run

The basic difficulty with this argument is the temporal character of hours. Let us first consider (for contrast) the more conventional situation where labor supply is cut back by reducing the *number* of workers through layoffs or dismissals. Most observers would agree that there are almost always some ways (with the possible exception of some continuous processes) in which capital can be substituted for labor, often because there is some slack in the use of labor that can be eliminated. In fact, if some overhiring had been practiced it may be possible to reduce the work force with little or no observable production loss.

Moreover, in the event of an economywide reduction in employment, labor may be transferred from one firm or industry to another which could possibly raise the capital-labor ratio. Such movement of labor among firms and industries (as well as within firms) would likely be toward capital-intensive processes. If a 25 percent cutback in labor meant a reduction of 25 percent in output in each sector, the financial cost to capital-intensive industry would certainly be greater because of the fixed costs (debt services, obsolescence, depreciation, maintenance, and so on) of holding great amounts of partially unemployed capital.

Another predicted shift from older to newer plants and production lines would have similar results. In each industry and in each large firm, machinery of quite different vintages is employed, but when labor is laid off, production can be concentrated on the more efficient machinery.

The situation differs, however, when we stop considering this more traditional case of varying the *number* of workers and analyze instead the effects of varying *hours* per worker. None of these methods of increasing the capital-labor ratio—that is, eliminating slack labor in the production process, shifting labor to capital-intensive industries, or concentrating production in the newer processes—is readily available when hours of work are reduced. Continue to assume full employment in the sense that both labor and capital are fully utilized. Let hours of work then be cut from forty to thirty hours a week. It follows that at any one time there are still as many people as before per machine. It is not clear that a reallocation of labor will raise its productivity. The only way in which the capital-labor ratio can be increased now is through the use of shiftwork—for example, by transferring day workers in labor-intensive processes to night work in capital-intensive industries. Of course, shiftwork is already used today, especially where the cost of capital is high relative to the cost of labor. (The important question of whether the use of shiftwork would, in fact, tend to be increased further as hours are reduced will be discussed later.) Apart from these potential gains from increases in the use of shiftwork, however, it is difficult to see how a reduction in hours of work would yield any significant gains in the capital-labor ratio in the short run.

In the Long Run

In the longer run, there is an opportunity for the size of the nation's capital stock to adjust to the new work schedules. Trade unions and other advocates of fewer hours of work have argued that capital will eventually be substituted for labor at an accelerated pace, so that little long-term reduction in output should be expected. However, it is more likely that a reduction in capital investment, not an increase, will result from a decline in hours of work.

The trade-union theory is essentially a generalization of experience at the firm or industry level applied to the economy as a whole. At this microlevel, when the supply of labor is reduced, which raises its relative price, capital is often substituted for labor, which raises the capital-labor ratio. But the financing for this investment in equipment comes out of the total investment funds available in the economy. If this national total is fixed, increased investment in one sector simply means less investment elsewhere. But if hours of work are reduced throughout the economy, there cannot be any compensatory increase in capital investment on an economywide basis. Capital investment can only be increased if the fund is increased. Hence, one should restate the question of whether capital can be substituted for labor to one of whether the aggregate supply and demand of investment funds would be increased by a reduction in hours.

In most models, the supply of funds for investment is based on the supply of savings (personal and corporate)—a function of the level of profits and, to a lesser extent, labor earnings. But both types of income would be reduced sharply by a reduction in hours of work. In a simple model in which investment is determined by domestic savings, we would predict that when hours of work are reduced, the capital-labor ratio would first rise because labor input was less. This ratio would then fall as the capital stock was diminished because output and, hence, savings and investment, were at lower levels. In some plausible models, the final result is that the capital-labor ratio is restored to its original level. For example, if a permanent reduction in hours of work from forty to thirty-two hours a week yielded a 25 percent net reduction in effective labor input, and if the long-term consequence was a reduction of capital stock by 25 percent from the level it would otherwise have reached, then it is plausible that national output would also be 25 percent lower.

Policies and Adjustments to Preserve Work Schedules

With all the possible negative impacts of reducing hours of work, what can be done to better meet employers' and employees' needs and still maintain our current level of employment and output? Certain government policy actions as well as those at the corporate level may allow the benefits of reduced hours without the difficulties.

Maintaining Full Employment

Avoiding long periods of persistently high unemployment is an excellent strategy for heading off a precipitous decline in hours worked. Prolonged economic depression eventually generates an ideology that work opportunities are limited. This in turn produces demands that work opportunities be shared equitably. The experience of the 1930s and subsequent years is that such restrictions are apt to become permanent, even after full employment has been restored. Demands for work sharing were muted for some years in this country. Then they became more insistent as unemployment levels crept upwards in the early 1970s. It is not implausible that a return to 1975 unemployment levels in this country might actually lead to national legislation mandating a reduction in hours of work.

Improving Incentives to Supply Labor

Governmental policies should be aimed at improving, not suppressing, individual incentives to supply labor to the market. A complementary factor encouraging workweek reductions is the so-called decline of the "work ethic." Attitudes toward work can affect both the hours and intensity of work performed. But the structure of financial incentives to work is certainly one of the factors influencing worker commitment. And equally obvious has been the trend in most areas of American life (including tax, welfare, and law enforcement policies) to reduce market incentives. A continuation of this trend could help to produce a reduction in working hours.

Improving Job Design and Working Conditions

Both the nature of work and employee job satisfaction were mentioned previously as being possible determinants of future reductions in hours of work. At the present time, specialists in personnel management have a wide variety of tools that some believe would make work more pleasant and satisfying to the typical employee. These tools range from outlays to improve the physical amenities of the workplace to a variety of changes in the work itself, which would be designed to improve its intrinsic interest—for example, job rotation, job enlargement, and matrix management.[11]

Reforming Work Schedules

Work schedules can be redesigned so that there will be less pressure to reduce the standard workweek. In the United States today, the average employee can set neither the timing nor the number of his or her hours. One result is that the forty-hour workweek becomes a binding constraint for millions of Americans. Forty hours may be a good *average* number, but employees vary widely in their needs, so that many find the standard workweek either too short or too long. Some individuals turn to the part-time labor market, to absenteeism, or to casual labor to shorten their hours; others seek moonlighting and overtime opportunities. The majority, however, find these alternatives to be unattractive and hence must tolerate the forty-hour schedule.[12]

A second basic scheduling problem arises because even those for whom the forty-hour workweek is acceptable typically find that their lack of control in the timing or "whenness" of their work provides a constraint. To some degree, the quality of household production, leisure, and work time are each depreciated by rigid scheduling practices. The most obvious case is the rush-hour commuter congestion caused by many enterprises establishing the same beginning and ending times of work. The providers of many professional services typically restrict their hours to the normal daytime schedule. Even some retail establishments still do this. Child care is also negatively affected. Families in which both parents work full time have a difficult time managing child care for their children, but if their schedules are rigid, their problem is considerably exacerbated. Leisure activity is also adversely affected by rigid work scheduling, at least indirectly. Crowded highways and beaches on summer weekends (or similarly crowded ski slopes on winter weekends) are obvious examples.

Rigid schedules, then, mean that workers are supplying "more" time, or at least a distribution of time that imposes more costs on

them than would hours freely chosen by themselves. There are
three basic methods for giving employees more choice in the timing
of their hours—namely, staggered hours, flexitime, and work modules.

Staggered Hours.   The first method, staggered work hours, provides one of the most elementary and most restricted types of flexibility. In a typical scheme, offices in a downtown area will agree to
change their closing hours from a common 5:00 P.M. to times rang-
ing from 4:45 P.M. to 5:15 P.M. at five-minute intervals. Corresponding changes are also made in opening hours. In an attempt to
reduce traffic congestion, the concept of staggered hours has been
introduced in a large number of the world's metropolises—for example, New York, London, Paris, Tokyo, and Washington.

Staggering hours does not have a negative impact on productive
interactions among a firm's employees since they all work the same
schedules. The principal advantage of the system is the contribution
it makes in reducing commuter congestion and in allowing the employee to commute under less stressful conditions. In addition,
employees are often given some voice in determining the timing of
the new schedule (voting as a group), which can bring less obvious
benefits. For example, it is quite common for employees to opt for a
somewhat earlier schedule, which allows for more daylight leisure
in the late afternoon.

Flexitime.   The new flexible hours-scheduling programs, popu-
larly known as "flexitime," provide a much greater degree of individual freedom. In a typical "pure" flexitime system, the employer
sets a "core" time during which all employees must be present—for
example, from 10:00 A.M. to 12 noon and 2:00 P.M. to 4 P.M. The
employer also sets a "bandwidth" within which all hours must be
worked—say, 6:00 A.M. to 6:30 P.M. In addition, certain restraints
must be imposed in the interest of the worker's health. For example, the employee may have to take at least forty-five minutes for
lunch and limit his or her hours to ten on any one day. The worker is
still required to put in the same total working time—say, an average
of forty hours a week. In the most limited variant, schedule flexibility is confined to daily starting and ending times, and the worker
must continue to put in a total of eight hours each day. In less
limited plans, the worker may vary his or her total daily hours. In
still more generous plans (more common in Europe than in the
United States), the employee may even carry hours forward from
week to week and month to month.

Flexitime is said to be enjoyed by 5 to 10 percent of the white-collar labor force in several European countries; in this country it is said to cover as many as two to three million employees. The advantages of flexitime to the employee are so obvious that the key question raised by flexitime is whether the system is consistent with the employer's productive efficiency. A number of empirical case studies[13] have found that flexitime and productive efficiency are indeed consistent. These studies have also found that employees generally prefer this system. For one thing, flexitime eases the commuting problem of the individual worker. Without having to worry about meeting a rigid schedule, employees no longer rush to work, which reduces the probability of an accident and eases anxiety and stress. Flexitime also allows easier access to retail outlets, service establishments, and government offices, which are open only during standard working hours. Workers report "more time" for managing child care and other family activities without reducing their workweeks—a benefit more commonly reported by employed wives.

Choice in the scheduling of hours can make an obvious contribution to resolving the time problems of the two-earner family, especially the problem of providing supervision for school-aged children. Some forms of flexitime even permit a working mother (or father) to take time off to tend to a sick child or handle some other emergency at home. These and other family advantages have been appreciated by employees. In fact, observers in Europe have pointed out that many workers (especially females) who could not otherwise manage a full-time job find that they can when offered the flexitime alternative.

Flexitime also brings about obvious advantages to those people trying to combine a job with a program of formal study. Many courses are offered only during the day. Moreover, even when courses are offered during the evening, the school may be at the other end of the metropolitan area from the individual's workplace. With flexitime, however, students can leave work early on the day or night they are attending classes.

Work Modules. A third method for giving employees some choice in work hours is based on computerization. Essentially, the schedule preferences of employees and the productivity needs of the enterprise are fed into a computer, which gives back a predetermined set of optimal schedules. Called work modules, this alternative offers a wide range of applications. For example, work modules might be used in a factory layout with two or three shifts of workers, where schedules for a very large work group must be determined simultaneously. The disadvantage of this method is the impracticality of feeding all the relevant information about individual preferences and company needs into the computer, so that a less refined result will necessarily be obtained than from the flexitime system. Nevertheless, the computerized system can be helpful in many situations in which the introduction of ordinary flexitime would be impractical. For example, we might think that individual scheduling would be impossible in a continuous-process industry operating on three daily shifts. But workers could vary their hours, which average eight per day and forty per week, only over a very long period of time (perhaps once a year). At the beginning of each year, workers would enter their preferences in the computer, and an optimizing result would be obtained (with ties broken by seniority). Whenever possible, each worker would be given his or her ideal schedule. Presumably, devoted skiers would have light schedules in the winter, while scuba divers would have vacations and long weekends in the summer.[14] In this way, a considerable degree of schedule flexibility could be offered even in a heavy manufacturing industry where it might otherwise appear to be impractical.

Permitting Choice Over Number of Hours Worked

Managerial experiments have concentrated on methods for giving employees a choice over the *timing* of hours, rather than providing more options on the *number* of hours. However, the rapid growth of the part-time job market has afforded considerable de facto choices over hours; further development of that market will probably give still more workers the option of choosing their hours of work in the years ahead.

The relatively low wages and status of part-time workers make this option unattractive to many employees. Insofar as these conditions simply result from managerial inertia (the virtually unanimous view of those working for legislation to improve the lot of the part-timer), the long-term prognosis for improvement is quite favorable—at least if there is anything to the economists' competitive theory of the behavior of the firm. But insofar as the poor treatment of part-timers is due to such objective factors as insufficient management incentives to train the part-timer or higher coordination and communication costs, the forecast is less clear.

Some specific improvements definitely could be made. For example, the training problem would be partly solved if trained, full-time employees were allowed to go on a part-time schedule when the need arose. Thus, when a woman became pregnant or had a small child to raise, when a young person wanted to return to school, or even when an older man wanted to reduce his work effort, they would be permitted to retain their position on a part-time basis. The coordination and communication problems could be minimized in two ways. One method would be through "job sharing," in which two workers share a job by dividing up the responsibilities in a manner that is convenient to both of them, by coordinating their own activities, and, of course, by sharing the income from the job. The second is based on the tendency of flexitime to organize compulsory interaction time around the "core" of the day. If flexitime is fully successful, then little would be lost if the part-timers were hired for just this core time.

Undoubtedly, management will come up with a number of potential methods of giving individuals more choice over the number of hours they work. It is not too implausible to predict that if a significant minority *does* come to want the thirty- or thirty-two-hour workweek, management ingenuity will develop new ways of accommodating this group without a general reduction to a four-day workweek for all employees.

Policies to Ease Adjustments to a Reduced Workweek

Proper government and private sector policies could mitigate the negative economic effects of a reduction in hours of work. It is quite true that the efficacy of such policies must depend on the scenario in which they are introduced. If hours are reduced for social reasons, despite widespread interest by individuals in maintaining their material living standards, the prognosis for success will be much better than if a four-day workweek is introduced simply because the average worker wants more leisure and is willing to make a substantial economic sacrifice to achieve it. But even in the latter case, it is unlikely that all workers would share this preference (as many today would prefer longer hours of work). In any event, it makes sense to begin preparing a package of policies that would be helpful in either eventuality.

Increasing Labor Force Participation

A thirty-hour workweek could permit higher labor force participation, but managerial policies must be designed to foster, not hinder, this result. For example, work times for all workers could be scheduled so they are convenient to married women. Perhaps the optimal schedule would be a workweek that coincided with the public school week.

Of course, this suggestion raises the whole issue of our present irrational system of school schedules (and so brings out the importance of changing public as well as private practices.) It is widely recognized that school schedules are well designed to meet the needs of agriculture for child labor in the summer but are otherwise an anachronism. A four-day workweek in the schools, combined with a 25 percent increase in the number of days attended per year, would permit the coordination of child and adult schedules if adult schedules were reduced to the thirty- or thirty-two-hour level.

Similarly, the present drive to end mandatory retirement would be congruent with company policies of deferring retirement by reducing hours for older workers to a level they can handle.

Maintaining or Improving Productivity and Capital Utilization

Higher labor productivity is always a desirable social goal, of course, but it will take on a particular importance to the economy if the supply of labor is reduced by a reduction in hours of work.

Some scheduling measures that might improve capital utilization if hours were reduced include shiftwork, part-time work, and overtime. For example, a three-day weekend shift of seven and one half to ten hours per day would enable capital utilization to be maintained without imposing any additional evening or night work. Other measures call for two 6-day, 6-hour-a-day shifts (for example, 6:00 A.M. to 12:00 noon and 12:00 noon to 6:00 P.M. In fact, a similar schedule proposal was adopted as a program by the women's division of the Swedish Social Democratic Party in the interests of furthering the sharing of household and market activities. However, this proposal runs counter to the tendency for leisure time modules to be increased, which we have observed in the United States and in other countries. (The proposal has *not* been adopted in Sweden.) Three 10-to-12-hour-a-day workweeks have also been suggested as another means of maintaining capital utilization.

Summary and Conclusions

Since World War II weekly hours of work have remained steady in contrast to the rapid decline in hours over the preceding forty years. Various factors have contributed to this, including the need of employees to work longer hours to maximize the benefits derived from costly education, both formal and informal.

A further reduction in hours may increase employment through job sharing, but the negative impacts to the employees in terms of a decline in real income or to the employers in terms of underutilization of capital may be evident as reduced investment and thus reduced productivity and output.

In the face of inflation and increased labor force participation of women, especially vis-à-vis child care, the standard forty hours is either too long or too short a workweek for many employees. Moreover, the inflexibility in the "whenness" of those hours presents problems. This can be seen by the rapid increase in workers who turn to part-time employment, whether it is in addition to or instead of full-time employment. Still, part-timers pay a cost through reduced income or reduced benefits that full-time employees do not.

Perhaps the resolution to the needs of both employers and employees is through flexible work schedules. The European examples seem rather successful, improving employee morale and yet maintaining hours per week and consequently output. This, tied with government policy changes that provide incentives to increase the supply of labor, can help ensure a more efficient use of our human resources in the 1980s.

Endnotes

1. Unless otherwise noted, data on hours of work and on employment are derived from two publications of the Bureau of Labor Statistics, *Employment and Earnings* and *Special Labor Force Reports*, and from the U.S. Bureau of the Census, *Current Population Reports*, Series P–50, 1947.

2. For statistical evidence on points 1 and 2, see Bornstein, Leon, "Industrial Relations in 1976: Highlights of Key Settlements," *Monthly Labor Review* (January 1977. 100, 1, pp. 27–35.

3. See John D. Owen, *The Price of Leisure* (Montreal: McGill–Queens University Press, 1970).

4. Richard A. Easterlin, *The Baby Boom in Historical Perspective* (New York: National Bureau of Economic Research, 1962). Cf. the discussion and empirical analysis in T. J. Kniesner, "The Full–Time Workweek in the United States, 1900–1970," *Industrial and Labor Relations Review* 30 (October 1976), pp. 3–15. Kniesner believes that rising female labor force participation has been another factor tending to increase hours of work.

5. For statements about the expected positive relationship between hours of work and investment in children, see T. A. Finegan, "Hours of Work in the United States," *Journal of Political Economy* 70 (October, 1962) pp. 452–470; Owen, (1970); C. M. Lindsay, "On Measuring Human Capital Returns," *Journal of Political Economy* (August 1971), pp. 1195–1215; and Y. Barzel, "The Determination of Daily Hours and Wages," *Quarterly Journal of Economics* 87 (May 1973), pp. 220–238.

6. See Jacob Mincer, "On-the-Job Training: Costs, Returns, and Some Implications," *Journal of Political Economy*, Supplement (October 1962). See also the discussion in Walter Y. Oi, "Labor as a Quasi-Fixed Factor," *Journal of Political Economy* 70, no. 6 (December 1962), pp. 538–55; Ronald G. Ehrenberg, *Fringe Benefits and Overtime Behavior: Theoretical and Econometric Analysis* (Lexington, Mass.: Lexington Books, 1971); Sherwin Rosen, "The Demand for Hours of Work and Employment," Proceedings of Conference on Work Time and Employment, (Washington, D.C.: National Commission for Manpower Policy, October 6–7, 1978); and M. S. Feldstein, "Specification of the Labour Input in the Aggregate Production Function," *The Review of Economic Studies* 34 (1967), pp. 375–86.

7. Cf. the discussion in Richard V. Burkhauser and John A. Turner, "A Time-Series Analysis on Social Security and Its Effect on the Market Work of Men at Younger Ages," *Journal of Political Economy* 86, no. 4 (August 1978), pp. 701–15. The authors argue that the operation of the Social Security system has already made a major contribution to the leveling off in hours and present empirical data to support this point.

8. Average annual rate of increase in output per unit of labor in the U.S. private domestic economy. John W. Kendrick, *Understanding Productivity: An Introduction to the Dynamics of Productivity Change* (Baltimore and London: The Johns Hopkins University Press, 1977), p. 31.

9. Ibid., p. 32.

10. This movement could also be supported by possible future gains in recreation technology. Although it may be unlikely that the recreation industry would be revolutionized by a drastic improvement of the type that occurred in the first decades of this century and helped to reduce hours in the 1900–1929 period. See Owen, *Price of Leisure*.

11. See Alvar O. Elbing, and John R. M. Gordon, "Self-Management in Emerging Flexible Organization," *Futures* 6, no. 4 (August 1974), pp. 319–28, for a discussion of how these reforms interact with work-scheduling processes.

12. Plus compulsory overtime when demanded.
13. For discussion of American experience, see First National Bank of Boston, "New Flexible Hours Increase Productivity at First National Bank of Boston," 1974; United States Social Security Administration, "Report on BDP Flexitime Study Midpoint Survey," Washington, D.C., 1974; Robert T. Golembiewski, Rick Hilles, and Munro J. Kagno, "A Longitudinal Study of Flexitime Effects: Some Consequences of an OD Structural Intervention," *Journal of Applied Behavioral Science*, 10, no. 4 (1974), pp. 503–32; William H. Holley, Jr., Archilles A. Armenakis, and Hubert S. Field Jr., "Employee Reactions to a Flexitime Program: A Longitudinal Study," *Human Resource Management*, 15 (Winter 1976), pp. 21–23; and M. G. Evans, "A Longitudinal Analysis of the Impact of Flexible Working Hours," *Studies in Personnel Psychology* 6, no. 2 (Spring 1975), pp. 1–11; Virginia Martin, *Hours of Work When Workers Can Choose* (Washington, D.C.; Washington's Business and Professional Women's Foundation, 1975); Virginia E. Schein, Elizabeth H. Maurer, and Jan P. Novak, "Impact of Flexible Working Hours on Productivity," *Journal of Applied Psychology*, 62, no. 4 (1977), pp. 463–65; Stanley L. Nollen and Virginia H. Martin, *Alternative Work Schedules. Part I: Flexitime* (New York: AMACOM, 1978); and Allan R. Cohen and Herman Gadon, *Alternative Work Schedules: Integrating Individual and Organizational Needs*, (Reading, Mass.: Addison-Wesley, 1978).

For a survey of European experience, see George Moller Racke, "The Effects of Flexible Working Hours," Ph.D. dissertation, University of Lausanne, Switzerland, 1975; Michael Wade, *Flexible Working Hours in Practice*, Essex: Gower, 1973; Stephen Baum and W. McEwan Young, *A Practical Guide to Flexible Working Hours* (London: Kogan Page, 1973); J. Harvey Bolton, *Flexible Working Hours* (Wembley: Anbar, 1971); Elbing and Gordon, Heinz, Allenspach, *Flexible Working Hours* (Geneva, Switzerland: International Labor Office, 1975); and Archibald A. Evans, *Flexibility in Working Life: Opportunities for Individual Choice* (Paris: Organization for Economic Cooperation and Development, 1973).

See David Plowman, "Flexible Working Hours—Some Labour Relations Publications," *The Journal of Industrial Relations* 19, no. 3, Sydney, Australia, (September 1977), pp. 307–313 for a useful survey of Australian experience.
14. I owe this example to Richard Dudek.

INDEX